Inazo Nitobe

The Intercourse Between the United States and Japan

an historical sketch

Inazo Nitobe

The Intercourse Between the United States and Japan
an historical sketch

ISBN/EAN: 9783337096694

Printed in Europe, USA, Canada, Australia, Japan

Cover: Foto ©ninafisch / pixelio.de

More available books at **www.hansebooks.com**

THE INTERCOURSE

BETWEEN

THE UNITED STATES AND JAPAN

AN HISTORICAL SKETCH

BY INAZO (OTA) NITOBE,

A. B. *(late professor)* (J. H. U.), A. M. and Ph. D. *(Halle)*, Associate Professor

---

BALTIMORE
THE JOHNS HOPKINS PRESS
1891

JOHN MURPHY & CO., PRINTERS,
BALTIMORE.

PREFACE.

In these days of universal intellectual activity, when each dawning day finds new literary productions brought to light, it requires an apology from an unknown novice in authorship, should he dare to trespass upon the patience of the public. My apology lies in the sincere gratitude I feel for the attitude of America, as a nation, towards Japan, and of a few individual Americans towards me personally. If this humble work of mine should contribute in the smallest measure toward strengthening the bond of national friendship, or serve to bring nearer to each other a few individual hearts in the two countries, I shall feel more than amply repaid for the time spent in writing the book.

I am well aware how far short of the possibilities of such a work this effort falls. If I had undertaken the task on a more elaborate scale, which might easily have been done with the materials which were placed at my disposal, I might, perhaps, have been able to succeed better; but I naturally shrank from imposing upon overburdened readers.

For the sources of my information I have depended firstly, on Japanese works of reliable authority; secondly, on foreign writers of different nationalities; and, thirdly, on personal correspondence with a number of Japanese and Americans, who took active part in the events which I have endeavored to describe. That they may recognize the identity of the author, who corresponded with them in 1885-87, let me state, that, owing to family affairs, my name has since been changed from "Ota" to "Nitobe." To all who have thus aided me, I cordially express my thanks.

The preparation of this monograph was undertaken with the encouragement of Professor Dr. Herbert B. Adams, while I was studying in the Johns Hopkins University during the years 1884–87. During the three years which have since elapsed, the MS. has remained untouched until I find myself again in the United States, on my way home from Europe. At Dr. Adams' suggestion, I have made some alterations and additions, and through his never-ceasing kindness I now offer it to the friends of Japan.

For valuable assistance rendered me in making emendations and in the reading of proof-sheets, I am under great obligations to my friend Mary P. Elkinton, of Philadelphia. Finally, I wish to express my indebtedness to the Friend under whose hospitable roof I have written a large part of this monograph.

INAZO NITOBE.

"EGERTON,"
Overbrook, Philadelphia, Pa.
10th month 17, 1890.

CONTENTS.

PAGE.

INTRODUCTION.

 Song of the Black Ship.. 1

CHAPTER I.—FOREIGN INTERCOURSE BEFORE PERRY.

 Traditional Foreign Intercourse.. 3
 Korea... 4
 China... 5
 Portugal.. 7
 Spain... 9
 Christian Persecutions... 11
 Exclusive and Inclusive Policy... 13
 England.. 16
 Holland.. 20
 Russia... 22
 France... 24
 Commercial Isolation not the Policy of Old Japan....................... 24
 Dawn of Western Knowledge in Japan..................................... 26
 The Political State of Japan in the Middle of the Century............. 28

CHAPTER II.—COMMODORE PERRY AND HIS AMERICAN PREDECESSORS.

 Early American Attempts at Negotiation................................ 31
 Commodore Biddle... 32
 Wrecks of Whalers.. 35
 A Curious Youth.. 37
 Service of the Whale in American-Japanese Intercourse.................. 37
 Causes of the Expedition... 38
 Just before the Expedition... 40
 Sketch of Perry's Life... 42
 What the World said of the Expedition.................................. 43

vii

	PAGE
Voyage of Perry's Squadron	45
The Squadron in Yedo Bay	46
The Shogunate at its Wit's End	48
The Spirit of the Times	49
Perry's Second Visit and Treaty	52
Synopsis of the Treaty of Peace, Commerce and Navigation, Signed at Kanagawa 31st March, 1854	53
Significance of the Treaty	54
Services of the Dutch	55
Legality of the Treaty	57
America Followed by Europe	59
Exchange of Ratifications	60

CHAPTER III.—DIPLOMACY AND COMMERCE.

American Disappointment in Regard to Perry's Treaty	61
Japan soon after Perry's Departure	62
American Pioneers of Commerce	63
Advent of Townsend Harris	64
Commercial Treaty	65
Treaty of Amity and Commerce	66
Growth of Treaty Ports	69
The Currency Question (1854–'69)	71
The Revival of Anti-Foreign Prejudice	75
Decline of Anti-Foreign Ideas	80
The Restoration of the Imperial Authority	84
The Shimonoseki Indemnity	86
Tariff Convention	88
Trade and Commerce	90
Japanese Exports to America	93
American Imports into Japan	96
Friendly Diplomacy	96
Extradition Treaty	100
Treaty Revision	102

CHAPTER IV.—AMERICANS AND AMERICAN INFLUENCES IN JAPAN.

Foreign Influences	110
Beginning with Perry	111
Townsend Harris in Yedo	113
Harris and Perry Compared	115

Educational Influence.. 116
Scientific Services... 123
Postal System.. 128
Religious Influences... 130
Agriculture.. 134
American Railways.. 137
Miscellaneous Services... 139
American Writers on Japan.. 141
Dark Side of Foreign Influences...................................... 151

CHAPTER V.—JAPANESE IN AMERICA.

Before Perry's Expedition.. 157
Shogun's Embassy... 160
Imperial Embassy... 162
Influx of Students... 165
Their Mental Aptitudes... 170
Morals... 173
Religion... 175
Romance.. 177
Female Students.. 179
Japanese in California... 183
Exhibitions, Mercantile Houses, &c................................... 185
Farewell... 189

A HISTORICAL SKETCH OF THE INTERCOURSE BETWEEN THE UNITED STATES OF NORTH AMERICA AND JAPAN.

INTRODUCTION.

SONG OF THE BLACK SHIP.

Thro' a black night of cloud and rain,
 The Black Ship plies her way—
An alien thing of evil mien—
 Across the waters gray.

Down in her hold, there labor men
 Of jet black visage dread;
While, fair of face, stood by her guns
 Grim hundreds clad in red.

With cheeks half hid in shaggy beards,
 Their glance fixed on the wave,
They seek our sun-land at the word
 Of captain owlish-grave.

While loud they come—the boom of drums
 And songs in strange uproar;
And now with flesh and herb in store,
 Their prows turn toward the Western shore.

And slowly floating onward go
These Black Ships, wave-tossed to and fro.

History begins with poetry, and the history of the American-Japanese intercourse is no exception to this general rule. Poetry is often prophetic and the ballad of the Black Ship is but an illustration of this fact. Forty or forty-five years ago, when the popular Japanese knowledge of the jet-black race as well as of the American nation, was as vague as the news of the lunar world, this seemingly nonsensical song resounded throughout the length and breadth of the land. The Empire of the Rising Sun was then in apparent peace and prosperity, or I might better say, in the words of Carlyle, "barren (of events), which, as Philosophy knows, is often the fruitfullest of all." There was no war, nor any rumor of war. The contented people could see nothing in the signs of the times—indeed, to them, there were no signs save those in the dockyards. There the number of shipwrights increased; at the long-neglected forts masons and carpenters were busy repairing, and filling their time of rest with the song of the Black Ship. But to the mind of a few statesmen and scholars this ballad foreboded "some strange eruption to our State." They were aware what the "Black Ships" meant and what kind of people manned them. "Let me make the ballads of the people," thought the unknown author of the *Black Ship*, "and let who will *un*make the laws."

Our relations with older foreign powers, and the consequent making and unmaking of the exclusion and inclusion laws, for which Japan had long acquired an unhappy notoriety, must engage our attention before we enter into the subject proper of *American-Japanese* intercourse. These relations I shall briefly sketch in the following chapter.

CHAPTER I.

Foreign Intercourse before Perry.

Traditional Foreign Intercourse.

Isolation, at least commercial isolation, was at no time the ultimate aim of the foreign policy of Japanese rulers. This was, as Commodore Perry shrewdly remarked, "in direct opposition to what history proved to be the natural temperament and disposition of the Japanese people."

It is unnatural and unlikely that a people mixed in race and inhabiting small islands not far from a continent, should long remain a hermit nation. Traditions seem to suggest that in times and places which history has not yet clearly disclosed to us, Japan was in communication with other countries. The old nursery story of Asaina's travels (about the first quarter of the thirteenth century), over unknown seas and to strange lands of pigmies and giants, as incredible as Gulliver's travels, has lately been connected with a temple in Mexico, where it is said antique armor very much like Japanese workmanship, is preserved in the Holy of Holies.[1] The amicable relations, which are believed to have existed in forgotten times (probably in the eighth century) between Persia and Japan, were a favorite subject of gossip a few years ago, when our government sent an envoy to that kingdom.

---

[1] For the abstract of the opinions of Neumann, D'Eichthal, &c., see Vining's *Inglorious Columbus*.

When we consider that during four years (1847–51) there were five foreign ships wrecked on our coast, and that from time to time many Japanese junks were cast ashore on the Pacific Coast of America,[1] it does not seem impossible, that in Alaska there should be a strong element of Japanese blood, or that Asaina, or any other pioneer, should visit South America, or that Hawaiians should be the degenerate descendents of the fugitive warriors of the Taira family, whom our history records as having been drowned after the battle of Danno-Ura (1185 A. D.).

Leaving these conjectures for future investigators to solve, let us now deal with the historically substantiated accounts of the subject.

Korea.

The year 157 B. C. is memorable in the history of our civilization, as the date of the visit of a Korean named Okara, and of the introduction of the art of writing by him. Later, in the year 33 B. C., a chronicle mentions that a boatful of Koreans arrived on the coast of Echizen. Six years later another party landed. Some of the geographical names of the province still indicate the sites where they permanently settled. The intercourse thus peacefully opened continued so, until the more ambitious Japanese made these neighbors their subjects. As the Koreans were remiss in paying tributes, a re-conquest was undertaken by the Empress Zingu in the third century A. D. The conquest was followed by the introduction of several arts into Japan and the immigration and naturalization of Koreans, as late as the seventh, eighth and ninth centuries. Their allegiance was again withdrawn, and was only renewed after the invasion of Taiko in the sixteenth

---

[1] See *Overland Monthly*, 1872, p. 353; also Bancroft, *Native Races of the Pacific Coast*, Vol. V, 51. Mr. Charles Wolcott Brooks, of San Francisco, made a special study of the subject. See his *Japanese Wrecks, Early Maritime Intercourse of Ancient Western Nations* and *Origin of the Chinese Race*.

century, who planned this expedition not so much for the
subjection of Korea as to make it a stepping-stone to the
acquisition of the Chinese Empire. The invasions and devas-
tations of Korea by the Japanese are said to have been the
main cause of the decline in her arts and sciences, and even
in the religion[1] of that kingdom. Our claim to Korea, like
that of the English kings to France, was a prolific source of
troubles, and it only ended in the treaty of 1876 (Feb. 27),
which recognized its independent sovereignty. This treaty
of amity and commerce, conducted by Count Kuroda, was a
reiteration in many respects of what Commodore Perry did
for our country in 1854. America opened Japan to the
world; Japan[2] opened Korea to America (American-Korean
treaty signed in 1882). The Korea of 1876 was like the
Japan of 1854. The one had to pass through the same vicis-
situdes of national regeneration as the other. The massacre
of the resident Japanese by conservative Korean mobs, in
July, 1882; the consequent indemnity of $550,000; the
remittance of a large part of this sum out of sympathy for
the struggling nation; the influx of Korean youths to Japan
for education—all these find their exact parallels in the history of American-Japanese relations, as we shall subsequently
see.

China.

A Chinese legend makes mention of one Sin-fu, who, in
the third century B. C., left the country in search of the elixir
of life. Ché-wang-té, a tyrant of the most atrocious type, was
then the monarch of the Celestial Empire. Having every con-
ceivable carnal pleasure, this despot longed for an eternal life,
that he might eternally enjoy its sensualities. Sin-fu inti-
mated that a panacea of immortality could be procured only

---

[1] Cf. Percival Lowell, *Chosön*, Boston, 1886, p. 184.
[2] Mr. Palmer, as early as 1849, predicted that only after the north-eastern
ports of China, Manchuria and Japan were opened, could Korea be brought
into the commercial world.

on Mount Fuji in Japan. He was appointed to lead the expedition to the mountain, and, with a train of three hundred lads and three hundred maidens, left China never to return. A Japanese chronicle speaks of the arrival of this party, and a spot is still marked in the province of Ki-i as the place where the explorer's bones rest. An enthusiastic Chinese author has recently attempted to identify Sin-fu with the founder of the Japanese Empire, and no less an authority than Frederick von Schlegel seems to entertain a similar belief.[1] But whatever the early connections between the two countries may have been in other ways, their first diplomatic intercourse began in the year 106 A. D. Now broken by quarrels, then again united by friendly bonds, with embassies dispatched to and fro, the two nations have been floating down the sluggish current of secluded life. The formal treaty between China and Japan was signed in September, 1871. Their neighborly feelings were sorely tried in the year 1873, on account of the massacre of some ship-wrecked Loo-Chooans in Formosa; in 1884 because of China's assumed sovereignty over Korea, and in 1886 regarding a riot of Chinese sailors in Nagasaki; but in each case matters were settled without coming into bloody conflict.

To the Chinese and the Koreans we owe many elements of our civilization as well as many of its later restrictions. Not only literature and science, art and industry, religion and philosophy, but also law and administration were all imported from one or the other of these countries.[2] Even the modern progress of Japan was, in its incipient stage, encouraged by Chinese influences. The fall of Nanking in 1644

---

[1] *Philosophy of History*, Eng. Trans. Bohn Library, p. 124. The author of Shan Hai King is of the same belief. See Vining's *Inglorious Columbus*, pp. 249, 250. Some Chinese writers would have Taipe as the founder of the Japanese imperial family in the thirteenth century B. C. See Neumann, *Ostasiatische Geschichte*, p. 59.

[2] The Chinese influences were most conspicuous in the sixth, seventh and eighth centuries. See the *Tokyo Independent*, Vol. I, Nos. 1, 2.

had the same effect[1] on Japan as that of Constantinople on Italy.

Portugal.

Marco Polo, the well known Venetian traveller, in his enterprising wanderings in the thirteenth century, came as far as the eastern coast of China, and in the court of Kublai Khan heard of Japan (Chi-pan-gu), which was, he says, "an island toward the east in the high seas, 1,500 miles distant from the continent."[2] He then speaks of the Great Palace, "which is entirely roofed with fine gold, just as our churches are roofed with lead," and also of the pavement and floors, which were "entirely of gold, in plates like slabs of stone, a good two fingers thick; and the windows also of gold, so that," he continues, "the richness of this palace is past all bounds and all beliefs." Marco Polo's account found its way to Genoa, where it was perused by Columbus; hence the notion of the great discoverer that he had reached Japan, when he landed on the island of Cuba. Both Marco Polo and Columbus, however, were denied the pleasure of visiting this El Dorado, and it was left for a Portuguese navigator to be the first of Europeans to reach it.

Fernao Mendez Pinto, while visiting all the islands discovered by his countrymen, quite accidentally[3] came upon Japan in 1542. A Japanese account of two arrivals of Portuguese about this time, is much confused. The marvellous narrative of Pinto himself does not throw much light upon the subject. Indeed, his name was ignobly immortalized by Cervantes, and

---

[1] This comparison can be developed to a great extent, with interesting and valuable results. Cf. Griffis, *Mikado's Empire*; Gutzlaff, *History of China*, Chap. XVII.

[2] See Yule, *Marco Polo*, Vol. II, p. 235.

[3] A writer in the *Blackwood's Magazine* (Vol. 85, p. 63) is "inclined to think that the meeting of the two peoples (Portuguese and Japanese) upon the coasts of China, would naturally lead the Portuguese to Japan. It is quite possible that until formal permission to trade was obtained from the Mikado and the Shogun, it was necessary to represent the visits as purely accidental."

"*Mendes*" passed as a synonym for "*mendaz*," liar. From various accounts it seems that the Chinese junk in which Pinto and his comrades were wandering about, steered to Tanegashima, where they were interrogated on landing as to the object of their coming. The Japanese put the question in Chinese characters on the sands of the beach, whereupon a Chinese who happened to be on board in the same manner wrote: "This is a foreign ship from the south-west (India, Cochin-China, or Manilla), come to trade with you." This was the first conference on record ever held between the Japanese and Europeans. The longest preserved souvenir left at this first interview with the Portuguese, was the gun,—the first fire-arm seen by the natives. So highly was it prized,[1] that Diego Zaimoto, a good marksman, was adopted by the governor of the place as a son, and so dexterous were the people in handicraft, that, according to Pinto, in six weeks they had made six hundred guns, and after fourteen years all the towns of the kingdom were abundantly provided with these arms.

Pinto's detailed and exaggerated reports attracted attention among his countrymen, both at home and abroad, and stimulated them to do likewise. It was from these reports, too, that Camoens[2] obtained his knowledge of Japan, of which he sings—

> "But most of earth is still from thee concealed,
> Until that period of futurity,
> When all the globe contains shall be revealed;
> Pass not unmarked the islands in that sea,
> Where Nature claims the most celebrity.
> Half hidden, stretching in a lengthened line
> In front of China, which its guide shall be,
> Japan abounds in mines of silver fine,
> And shall enlighten'd be by holy faith divine."

---

[1] The Japanese word *teppo* (gun) is a corrupt form of *cho-ho*, literally excellent treasure.
[2] *The Lusiad*, Canto X: cxxxi. Eng. trans. by Robert F. Duff.

Pinto's pioneer voyage was followed by others. The new commerce proved after a while quite lucrative. It was patronised by the feudal princes of Southern Japan, as it furnished them with efficient weapons and costly luxuries. Medicines and woven fabrics were the principal imports. Gold was abundant and cheap in Japan. There were as yet no coinage regulations, and the relative value of gold as compared with silver and copper was exceedingly low; hence gold bullion formed the chief item of export. The quantity of precious metals, with a large preponderance of gold, exported from 1550 to 1639, is estimated at fifty-nine and a half millions sterling, or an annual average of three and one-third million dollars.[1] The traffic was carried on in the harbor of Hirado; but, at the suggestion of the Portuguese, after 1566 [2] Nagasaki was the centre of foreign trade.

Tobacco [3] and potatoes [4] were also introduced by the Portuguese, whose services to Japan were chiefly of a material nature, differing in this respect from the almost exclusively religious character of the relations which Spain had with our country.

Spain.

The Spanish merchants had been covetous of the good fortune of their Iberian neighbor in obtaining the favor of the Japanese, and they also applied for advantages of trade. These were granted without any difficulty. So jealous were the Spaniards of the Portuguese monopoly, that at one time (1591) they

---

[1] Meylan estimates the annual export of metals, almost entirely of copper, at £660,000, while Kämpfer speaks of some years when they exported £2,500,000. Cf. Dr. Geerts, Trans. of Asiatic Soc. of Japan, IV, 91.

[2] Some say 1570. Only after it was fixed as an anchorage of foreign ships, has Nagasaki grown in importance. Till then it was only a small fishing hamlet. Cf. W. A. Woolley, Trans. of Asiatic Soc. of Japan, IX, 125.

[3] See Satow's account of the introduction of the weed in Trans. of Asm. Soc. of Japan, VI, 68.

[4] Cocks claims that he was the first to plant this tuber in Japan. Diary, I, 11. It is known as "Jacatra tuber" in Japan.

even denounced the Portuguese Jesuits to the Shogun. As has been said, the relations between Spain and Japan partook more of a religious than a commercial character. In 1534, Ignatius Loyola founded his order of Jesuits and, with the vitality of a fresh organization, the Society was propagating and proselyting in every direction. Francis Xavier was preaching on the Malabar Coast, when the intelligence of Pinto's visit to Japan was brought to him. A Japanese youth by the name of Paul Anjiro (Hanshiro?),[1] on account of a homicide he had committed, had fled from the country, and on board Pinto's junk made his way to Macao and thence to Goa, where, under the great Jesuit's influence, he was converted to Christianity. It was doubtless at his suggestion that Xavier, with his two colleagues, hastened to the new field, reaching it in 1549. Possessed of talents of the highest order, of courage and zeal unsurpassed, of purity of character, he was a man preëminently fit for a pioneer missionary in any land, at any time. But if we add to these personal qualities of the man, the almost irreligious state of the populace, the absence of "insolent Mohammedans and filthy Jews," and the assurance of protection from Nobunaga the Shogun of the time, we can easily see why it was that he and his successors reaped within twenty years a harvest of 300,000[2] souls in the highest and lowest walks of life, and built more than forty churches and monasteries besides several chapels. Xavier stayed only about two years, and returning to Shan Shan, near the Canton river, there died in 1552. The strong affection he felt for the Japanese people is evident from his own words: "I cannot cease from praising these Japanese. They are truly the delight of my heart."

---

[1] He came in 1547 to Malacca and was baptized under the name of Paulus de Santa-fé.—Beer, *Geschichte des Welthandels*, Bk. IV, Chap. 4.

[2] Some authority gives the number of converts in 1582 at 200,000 and of churches 250. In 1605 there were 1,800,000 professors of the Christian religion.

Attracted by the spiritual fertility of the soil, swarms of reapers who had no share in sowing—friars of all sects[1]—soon found their way to the field. The Spanish religious orders were chiefly Franciscan,[2] the Portuguese, Jesuit. In geographical distribution the Dominicans were in Satsuma, the Franciscans in Yedo, the Jesuits in the Capital and southern provinces. As their labors grew brisker, different orders jostled one another, and the house would have been permanently divided against itself, were it not for the persecution that befell them alike and for a time united them.

Christian Persecutions.

The impetuous character of the native converts, the ingratiating acts and the popularity of papists among the masses, the domineering behavior of the priests, their claim to miraculous powers, the novel doctrine that there was a king of kings to whom allegiance was primarily due, and that the vicar of this king did actually reign in Rome—these would have been enough to rouse the jealous susceptibilities of any ruler; but when to these was added a slur on the authority of the State, or an attempt at conspiracy, it is not to be wondered that a religious persecution, which had never before disgraced the fair land of Nippon with the blood of her children, for the first time became a sad fact in her history.

The immediate cause of the persecutions, beginning in 1585 under Hideyoshi (Taiko) and continuing through the times of Iyeyasu and his successors, is not exactly known, so diverse are the accounts on this point. According to one narrator, a paper containing a scheme of conspiracy formed among the

---

[1] The Bull of 1608, issued by Pope Paul V, allowed free access to Japan of religious of all orders. See John H. Gubbins, *Review of the Introduction of Christianity in China and Japan*, Trans. Asiatic Soc. of Japan, Vol. VI, and learned observations on it from native and European sources by Satow, pp. 43–62 in the same volume.

[2] They first came from the Phillipines in 1593.—Adams' *Hist. of Japan*, 63.

Christian converts against the Shogun, was intercepted on its way to Lisbon, by a Dutch vessel, in 1613.[1] A second writer (Kämpfer) states that the circumstance which precipitated the persecution occurred in 1596, when a bishop, in meeting a native grandee on the high road, ignored the established act of courtesy which required the prelate to alight from his sedan and pay his respects to the nobleman. Still another authority[2] gives the following instance as the immediate cause of persecution: A Spanish naval officer, in a public entertainment at Nagasaki, boasted that his sovereign was the mightiest monarch of the world, and spreading out a map he pointed to the Spanish dominions in both hemispheres. "How is it possible," asked a lord of the court, who was among the listeners, "that your king can obtain possession of so many foreign countries?" "Ah, that is easy enough," answered the Spaniard, "he sends the missionaries, in the first instance, to any kingdom he wishes to conquer; for some years they preach and make converts, and then, when the Christians are powerful enough, they drive out the reigning sovereigns and bring in the king of Spain." Turanus Vekitis (English translation in *Japan Weekly Mail*, December 27, 1884), in his little book, published in Antwerp, 1628, attributes the cause of Hideyoshi's persecution to the following fact: While the project of Korean invasion was going on, it was found desirable to obtain some large vessels for the conveyance of the troops. Just then a Dutch (?) ship was at anchor at Hirado. Hideyoshi requested the captain to have it sent to Takata, Bungo. The great draught of the vessel made it impossible for him to comply with the request. The same night this occurred, orders were sent to the fathers to depart from the country within twenty days. According to Father Franciscus Solierus, a certain court physician tried to seduce some Christian maidens for

---

[1] See Page's *Hist. de la Religion Chrétienne au Japon*, Vol. I, 450.

[2] Lady Fullerton, *Laurentia*, an interesting story of a Christian maiden in Japan, lately republished in the Tauchnitz Edition.

the pleasure of his master. Failing in this, he slandered the
Christians.

The Jesuits' accounts, as given in Charlevoix's History,
attribute the immediate cause of persecution to the intrigues
of the English and Dutch traders. Mr. Gubbins (*Asia. Soc.*,
VI, 30) is inclined to attribute to Buddhism an important share
in instigating the persecution of Christians.

Whichever of these was the real cause, the years of Hideyoshi and Iyeyasu's domination saw the banishment of native
converts, the expulsion of foreign ecclesiastics, and the sum-
mary trials and wholesale slaughter which rival in horror the
fires of Smithfield or the rack of the Inquisition.[1] These outrages gave rise in turn to the revolt of Shimabara in 1637,
where 30,000 Christian peasants took arms against the persecutors. This revolt was extinguished in the blood of the
insurgents, and Catholicism disappeared from our national
life, surviving till the present era only in some of the retired
villages.

Exclusive and Inclusive Policy.

On the ground that all the Spaniards and Portuguese were
followers and allies of "the evil sect," they were ordered to
leave forever the sacred soil of the divine land.[2] It is recorded
that as many as two hundred and eighty-seven men and
women of Portuguese extraction were taken to Macao. Before
the close of 1639, there was left neither a missionary nor a merchant of either of these nationalities, except some few who
were naturalized or who apostatised.[3] Thus was consummated

---

[1] The Catholic martyrology of Japan is still an untouched field for a historian. Several authentic and contemporary MSS. are said to be extant in
secret keeping. From Dr. Ernst Satow's pen is to be expected new light
on the subject, as he is engaged in research in European monasteries and
libraries.

[2] Japan as called by Shinto zealots.

[3] It is interesting to read in Gibbon that almost simultaneously the same
thing was taking place in quite another part of the world. His words

by Iyeyasu the *exclusive* measures so jealously maintained by his successors for two centuries and a half. His policy did not stop here. It was as *inclusive* as it was exclusive.[1] So rigorous was the edict of 1637, that not only were foreigners forbidden to land on the Japanese coast, but the natives were forbidden to leave it. After 1609, ships above a certain tonnage (500 koku = 2,500 bushels or 30,000 cu. ft.) were not allowed to be built, the motive of this legislation being to cripple distant navigation. Prior to this period, there had been free exits of the natives, and necessarily ship-building had been carried to quite a high degree of perfection, as fragments of old naval architecture show. The adventurous spirit of the people often drove them from their narrow island home.

A little before the above law was passed, many bold spirits had sought in other lands a wider field of gain, achievement and fame.[2] One (Tenjiku Tokubei) steered a course to Hindostan. A merchant of Nagasaki (Tsuda Matazaimon) had a princess of Siam given him in marriage for the service he had done in a war with Goa. Another Japanese (Yamada Nagamasa) made his way to Siam, and for his military valor was made a governor of two of its provinces.[3] In 1583, the two southern princes of Arima and Omura despatched an envoy

---

describe the state of Japan as appropriately as they do that of Æthiopia.— "The monophysite churches resounded with a song of triumph, 'that the sheep of Æthiopia' were now delivered from the hyænas of the west; and the gates of that solitary realm were forever shut against the arts, the science and the fanaticism of Europe." (*Decline and Fall*, Ch. XLVIII).

[1] Inclusive policy is by no means an oriental statecraft. For political reasons, Washington did not relish the idea of sending American youths to the monarchical countries of Europe, while, for economic reasons, all intercourse with foreign nations was to be narrowly watched in Babœuf's ideal commonwealth.

[2] Cf. Hildreth, *Japan as she was and is*, 556.

[3] The intercourse with Siam was most lively in the first quarter of the seventeenth century. In some of its towns Japanese colonies were founded. Cf. E. Satow, *Notes on the Intercourse between Japan and Siam*, Trans. Asiatic Soc. of Japan, Vol. 13, p. 139.

consisting of four persons of rank to the Roman Pontiff. After they had been three years on the way, they arrived in Lisbon, and passing through Spain reached Rome, where they were cordially welcomed by Gregory XIII. They were still in the Holy City when the Pope died. At the coronation of his successor, Sixtus V, they were knighted. They travelled through Central Italy, fêted everywhere.[1] It was after eight years of absence that they returned home, taking with them a reinforcement of seventeen missionaries. In 1613, while the persecution was hotly raging, Daté, a prince of a large province in the East, secretly despatched his vassal, Hashikura, to Rome. A man of daring ambition, Daté looked beyond the narrow precincts of Japan for the sphere of his activity. Hashikura was advised to place himself in the centre of European politics and watch their movements; in a word, he was sent as a spy. Thrown amidst religious influences, he soon deserted his worldly master and professed himself a Christian proselyte. He was given knighthood by the Pope, but on his return home in 1620, as a reward of his conversion, he was put to death.

Many had been the ships that plied between Java, Manilla, Annam, Siam, Malacca, China, Corea and India in those times;[2] but all these enterprises were ended by the inclusive legislation. Jealous of foreign influences as Iyeyasu was, he was not a man to be blinded by race or religious prejudices.[3] His suspicion of the Catholics did not influence him greatly

---

[1] In Venice are still to be seen, among the pictures of the Doges, the paintings of these Japanese. This embassy formed the precedent of the special envoy, Mgr. Osouf, sent by the Holy See to the Court of the Mikado in September, 1885. Cf. *The Month*, Dec., 1886.

[2] See J. M. James on *Foreign Travel of Modern Jap. Adventurers*, based on the native accounts of Kai-Gai-I-den (1860), Trans. of Asiatic Soc. of Jap., VII, 191.

[3] When one foreign nation calumniated another, Iyeyasu answered "Even if a devil should visit my country from hell, he shall be treated like an angel from heaven."

in his dealings with foreigners who were not Romanists, as we see in the instances of the Dutch and the English.

Thus, cut off from the rest of the world by this exclusive and inclusive policy, there was established a society impervious to foreign ideas from without, and fostered within by all sorts of artificial legislation. This legislation affected every department of private and public life. Methods of education were cast in a definite mold; even matters of dress and household architecture were strictly regulated by the State. Industries were restricted or forced into specified channels, thus retarding economic development. As no relations existed with foreign powers, international wars did not occur. Peace reigned within the Empire; but only such peace as would be possible in the slumber of the Middle Ages. If, however, in the Middle Ages clouds were gathering to burst amid the thunder and lightning of the Renaissance and the Reformation, so was it in Japan, that, in spite of political and economic inactivities, the Tokugawa period was pregnant with mighty forces—forces which, as we shall see, were soon to reveal themselves in the awakening life of the New Era—the Era of the Restoration.

England.

The first mention that we have of any English vessel in our waters was in 1564, when one entered a port in Hizen. Nothing further than her arrival is recorded. Sixteen years later another entry was effected, this time to Hirado. Agreement was made with the people to trade, and for successive years the port was frequented. English commerce did not, however, take any firm footing until some years later.

In April, 1600, a Dutch ship—one of a fleet of five sail bound for the East Indies—after meeting with calamities on the coasts of Guinea and Chili, steered for Japan. She had a cargo of woolen goods to dispose of. This was an evil time for any foreigner, but especially for the English, and that in a Dutch ship, to come to Japan. The Portuguese merchants held tenaciously their monopoly of Japanese trade, and their compatriot religionists persistently denounced the English and the Dutch as sworn heretics. The pilot of the ship was a Kentish man, William Adams[1] by name, and when the crew landed in Bungo, he, as spokesman, was carried in company with one other to the court of Osaka, where, through a Portuguese interpreter, "the king (Iyeyasu)," to quote his own words, "demanded of what land I was, and what moved us to come to his land, being so far off. . . . Then the great king asked whether our country had wars? I answered him, yea with the Spaniards and Portugals, being in peace with all other nations. Further he asked me in what I did believe? I said in God that made heaven and earth. . . . Two days after he sent for me again and inquired of the qualities and conditions of our countries, of wars and peace, of beasts and cattle of all sorts, of heaven and stars. It seemed that he was well content with mine answers." So well content indeed was the "king" that Adams was prevailed upon by him to give up all hope of returning home. "My wife is in a manner a widow, and my children fatherless, which only thing is my greatest grief of heart and conscience." Meanwhile, his frank, straightforward character, his Protestantism, his knowledge of geometry, mathematics and ship-building, made him a great favorite with Iyeyasu. "Now, for my service which I have done, and daily do, being employed in the emperor's (Shogun's) service, he hath given me a living like unto a lordship in England, with eighty or ninety husbandmen, who are my servants and slaves.[2] The precedent was never done before. Thus God hath provided for me, after my great misery; to His name be the praise forever. Amen."

---

[1] Cf. *Dictionary of National Biography*, Art. Adams. See also Rundall's *Memorials of the Empire of Japan*, Hakluyt Society publication.

[2] Adams did not mean *slaves* in the usual acceptation of the term; for there was no system of slavery in Japan.

This "lordship" was located in Himemura (Princess Village), not far from Yokohama. Adams was made a *samurai* with the Japanese name Anjin (Pilot) Miura (which was the name of the county he lived in), and a house-lot was given him in Tokyo (then Yedo), the street in which it stood being still called Anjin-Cho (Pilot Street).[1]

The English trade assumed a definite form on the arrival of Captain Saris, in 1613. He was furnished with a letter and presents from James I to Iyeyasu. With Adams' assistance Saris succeeded in obtaining very liberal privileges of trade.[2] The factory which he started in Hirado was left, at his return, in charge of nine Englishmen, with Richard Cocks[3] as director.

By this time the English and the Dutch entirely superseded the Spaniards and the Portuguese in the field of commerce. The English had their establishments in many places, as Yedo, Osaka, Fukui, Kochi, Fukuoka, Karatsu, Suruga, Higo, Hakata, Sakai, Nagasaki, Hirado, &c.; hence it was a tremendous blow when, in 1616 (the year in which Iyeyasu died), a proclamation was passed that "no Japon should buy any merchandize of strangers," except at Hirado. About a year after this proclamation, Cocks makes the following entry in his *Diary* under date of September 10, 1617 : " I had much conferrance with hym (king of Firando) about our busyness, namely how we should procead to have our privilegese enlarged that were shortened the yeare past; unto which he promised his assistance, willing us, as Semi Dono did the lyke, to geve out the worst speeches we could of the Hollanders, that it might com to themperours ears." Circumscribed in their privileges, deprived by death of some of its members,

---

[1] There is a street in Tokyo called "Ya-yō-su," said to be so named from a Dutchman, who had a residence in that quarter. I could not find any name that sounds like it, except, perhaps, it be "Johann Yossen," of whom account is given in Cocks' *Diary*. An imperfect way of pronouncing foreign words, and the common practice of abbreviating names may have given rise to Ya-yō-su from Johann Yossen.

[2] Hawks' *Japan Expedition*, 43–45.

[3] His *Diary* throws a flood of light on the inner working of the factory.

and with a zealous competitor—the Dutch—at its side, the English factory was found a losing concern. Besides, a company—a "ring" of native merchants—appeared in the market.¹ After expending about £40,000, the East India Company, under whose auspices the Hirado factory was conducted, decided in the Council of Batavia, in 1623, to withdraw from the country.² This left the Dutch the sole agents of European commerce. The English, however, did not give up the idea of regaining their foothold, and, in the course of the following fifty years, the question of again establishing a factory in Japan, was debated five times, and thrice were ships sent out for the purpose. In 1637, an ominous year, a fleet under Lord Weddel touched at Nagasaki, where an unsuccessful attempt was made to open negotiations.³ In 1673, appeared the *Return* in the harbor of Nagasaki; Charles II's royal message, which she conveyed, asked for the renewal of commerce on the basis of the old agreement. The proposal was subjected to consultation with the Dutch residents, and their reply that the English monarch had lately married a Portuguese Infanta (Catharine of Braganza) was sufficient to make the Japanese give a negative answer at once. The hostilities in which England was engaged with Holland, will partly account for this unsuccessful issue of her mission. In 1681 and 1683, indirect futile attempts were made to open negotiations, through the mediation of the princes of Bantam, Amoy, Taiwan, Tonquin and Siam.⁴

¹ The Englishman, Cocks, does not quite like this "ring." See his *Diary*, II, 322. If he had studied the history of his own country, he would have found an exactly parallel case in the company of Merchant Adventurers, in the time of Henry VIII, which drove the Hanseatic merchants from the market. See Philp, *The History of Progress in Great Britain*, II, 99.

² The alleged reasons for this withdrawal were the danger of the seas between Japan and Batavia, the small hopes of procuring trade with China and the loss of a ship laden with commodities destined for Japan. Cf. Cocks' *Diary*, II, 346.

³ Fraser, *Magazine*, Vol. XXXIV (1846), 701.

⁴ Cf. Cocks' *Diary*, I, xlviii. See W. G. Aston on H. M. S. "Phaeton" at Nagasaki in 1808, *Trans. Asiatic Soc. of Jap.*, VII, 323, translated to a great extent from Japanese account.

Holland.

Mention has already been made of the first Dutch vessel that anchored in the bay of Sakai-ura, in 1600. The object of this voyage being ascertained beyond doubt to be purely mercantile, the Hollanders were granted letters patent. In July, 1609, they came again and were allowed to settle in the port of Hirado. It was not, however, till two years afterward that Jacob Speck arrived, and, through the good offices of William Adams, received the most favorable terms for trading. From Hirado the Dutch were transferred in 1641 to Deshima,[1] an island in front of Nagasaki. This place had just been emptied by the expulsion of the Portuguese. Eight, subsequently two, and still later one, was the number of Dutch vessels that, according to terms of agreement, yearly visited from Batavia these voluntary exiles. The exports consisted chiefly of copper,[2] gold,[3] silver,[4] tea, silk, bronze, camphor, and tobacco (?), which the Dutch disposed of in Batavia at 50

---

[1] A good parallel to the life in Deshima, was the Hanseatic Steelyard in London. Compare Kämpfer with Pauli's *Pictures of Old England*, Chap. VI.

[2] In the seventeenth and eighteenth centuries copper was rare. The exportation began in 1644, but its annual amount was limited by law to 15,000 piculs in 1714, and to 10,000 in 1721. It is calculated that 206,253 tons of copper were exported by the Dutch during the period from 1609 to 1858. See Rein, *Japan*, Eng. trans., 335.

[3] Vincent Romyn, and afterwards William Verstegen, who visited Deshima, sent a memorial after returning to Batavia (about 1635) to the Gov. Gen. Henricus Bromver, stating the great importance for the East India Company to commence a trade with the Gold and Silver Islands, situated in the Pacific Ocean at 37½° N. Lat. The Dutch sent two vessels in 1639 and again in 1643, in search of these precious islands. The gold export in the seventeenth century by the Dutch, is valued at 6,192,900 pieces of the old Koban. The total value of gold and silver taken out of the country by the Dutch in the seventeenth century, is estimated at 43,482,250 pounds sterling. According to Sir Stamford Raffles, in the 200 years (1540-1740) Japan must have been drained of bullion to the value of 200,000,000 dollars. Cf. Dr. Geerts, *Trans. of Asiatic Soc. of Japan*, IV, 90-92; Leon Levi, *Hist. of British Commerce*, 383.

[4] The exportation of silver was prohibited in 1671. Exportation to China was restricted, in 1685, to 4,968,000 pounds.

per cent. profit. The total amount of metal (copper?) exported by the Dutch during 249 years (1609-1858), is calculated at 4,209,500 piculs. According to native account, the amount of gold exported 1648-1708 was about 2,397,600 rio, of silver, 374,429 kwamme. Copper was exported, 1663 to 1707, to the amount of 1,114,498,700 kin. The free efflux of the precious metals in large quantities from the country, called forth memorials from the economists and financiers of the time, and restrictions were imposed on such exportation. This fact, together with the frequent debasement of coins since 1696, made the Dutch trade less and less profitable; so much so that, whereas, previous to 1743, the annual gross profits had been as high as $200,000, they fell after that time to $80,000. Still the Dutch never quitted the land, whose products they monopolized for European markets. Deprived of their rights, nay, of the noblest rights for which their countrymen were fighting at home,—namely, liberty of conscience; despised as an inferior people, confined and watched, these patient Hollanders, twenty or so in number, carried on their painful toil. Literally were the words of the poet fulfilled,—

"E'en liberty itself is bartered here,
At gold's superior charms all freedom flies."

Kämpfer himself does not deny the humiliation of his countrymen.

In this way the Dutch remained faithful to our country. When the Catholic revolt of Shimabara was raging, it was the Dutch who warned the Shogun that the Portuguese king was preparing to equip eight men-of-war, to give assistance to the Christian insurgents.[1] As we have seen, it was the Dutch, too, who dissuaded us from renewing commercial rela-

---

[1] Not only that, they even supplied the persecutors with ammunition. It is said that M. Kockebecker, director of the Hirado factory, repaired to Shimabara, and within a fortnight battered the town with 426 balls (Davis, China, II, 267).

tions with England. It was their king, William II,[1] who, in a most friendly letter, cautioned the Shogun in 1844, by reflections upon the Opium War and its consequences in China, to be prepared for defence, or, preferably, to open the country to foreign trade. It was the Dutch who, in 1852, told our government of America's plan to send an expedition, and again, in 1853, advised us to be more cordial and civil to foreign nations. Thus, if St. Petersburg was, as its illustrious founder said, a window through which Russia looked upon Europe, the little isle of Deshima, well and prophetically signifying "Fore-Island," was Japan's window, through which she looked at the whole Occident.

Aside from foreign intelligence, we are under obligation to Holland for the arts of engineering, mining, pharmacy, astronomy and medicine. Especially for the last are we greatly indebted to her. "Rangaku"[2] (*i. e.*, Dutch learning) passed almost as a synonym for medicine; but more of this elsewhere.

The formal treaty, abrogating the many restrictions on their trade and raising the Netherlands to the level of other European powers in the estimate of Japan, was signed on January 30, 1856.

Russia.

To Russia, aspiring to maritime power and yet denied the gift of harbors of any account, the neighboring island empire of Japan is an eye-sore.

In 1700 Kamtchatka was for the first time known to the Russians. Thirty-six years later, Spagenburg made a voyage to the southern isles of the Kurile group. The fertile Island of Hokkaido (Yesso), of which the Kurile group is but a

---

[1] The letter is dated February 15. See v. Siebold, *Urkundliche Darstellung der Bestrebungen von Niederland und Russland zur Eröffnung Japans für die Schiffahrt und den Seehandel aller Nationen.* Bonn, 1854, pp. 5, 6, 9, 10.

[2] The history of Dutch learning in Japan has been written by K. Mitsukuri, *Trans. Asiatic Soc. of Japan*, V., Part I, 207; also by Y. Fukuzawa, *Tōkyō Independent*, 1886.

geological continuation, presented a fascinating contrast to the bleak plains of Siberia. Likewise were the reports of the main island so tempting, that the Russians would make every effort to open Japan; first for its commerce and religion, and finally for the parade ground of her Cossacks. Late in the last century, a Japanese vessel was wrecked on one of the Aleutian Islands, but the crew was rescued and, after being detained ten years, was kindly sent back, upon advice of Queen Catherine II.[1] Lieutenant Laxman, son of the celebrated Professor Laxman, who was employed in this errand of mercy, sailed from Okotsk in 1792. He entered the harbor of Hakodate, but being refused landing soon left. The Emperor Alexander renewed, in 1804, the effort to open intercourse. Resanoff, the special embassador on the occasion, landed in Nagasaki and, after tedious delays and polite mortifications, received an answer that "all communications between you and us are impossible." Indignant, he left, and on his way home gave vent to his feelings by inciting two Russian naval officers to make a hostile landing on the Japanese Coast. This they did, plundering some poor fishermen's villages in the North.[2] The capture of Golownin, in 1811, was a measure of revenge for the outrages of Chivostoff and Davidoff, who committed the above depredations.

Many attempts were subsequently made on the part of the Russian government to obtain a foothold on Japanese soil, but they failed every time, until after the precedent set by the United States. The treaty of peace and friendship was signed on February 7, 1855.

For Russia the Japanese have had no reason to entertain a very favorable feeling. The Kurile Islands, which had belonged to Japan, were slowly and silently wrested from

---

[1] Under the great queen's patronage, even a professorship of the Japanese language was started in Irkutsk.

[2] This took place in 1906 and 1907. An account is related by W. G. Aston, *Trans. of Asiatic Soc. of Japan*, I, 86–95.

our territory, or, as the native phrase is, "were moth-eaten." The constant boundary disputes in Saghalien, which it was a policy becoming the aggressive temper of Russia to evoke, only terminated in the exchange of that island in 1875, for a comparatively useless group of the Kuriles.

France.

When Colbert took upon himself the responsibility of creating order out of financial chaos, he projected a mission to Japan, and caused memorials to be drawn up for that purpose by Francis Caron, who had once served in the Dutch factory at Nagasaki.[1] The well known foresight of Colbert is also manifest in his proposition that only the Protestant subjects of Louis XIV should be brought in contact with the government of Japan. His plan was not carried out.

In 1846, Admiral Cecille undertook the part of a rival diplomat against Commodore Biddle. They were equally unsuccessful, and the treaty of amity and commerce was not signed until October 9, 1858.

Commercial Isolation not the Policy of Old Japan.

From what has been related, it may be inferred that it was never a policy of Japan to isolate herself from the commercial brotherhood of nations. What she feared was a political interference and even danger to her very existence as a state. It was a Monroe doctrine in its aggressive shape, and as such contained a grain of wisdom. Instead of being content to be *excluded* from the world and *included* within the narrow precincts of their native land, our people were anxious to take an active part in business of international scope.

The adventurous spirit of the islanders often drove them from their seclusion. The easy assent to the proposals of

---

[1] Hildreth, *Japan as it was and is*, p. 571.

mutual trade, the license readily granted to missionaries for the preaching of a new religion, the kind treatment of foreigners wrecked on our coast—all tend to show that it was not in the nature of our people to be Ishmaelites, with their hand against the world and the world's hand against them.

It is in their antagonism to Roman Catholicism, or rather to Roman Catholics, that we can find the main cause of our exclusive policy. Economic reasons against foreign trade were a complaint of a later period: neither did European politics[1] or state-systems directly influence the inception of our exclusive legislation.

Dawn of Western Knowledge in Japan.

Allusion has already been made to the spread of the Dutch studies. Eager students in the beginning and middle of this century flocked from all quarters to Nagasaki, to study nautical art, military tactics, materia medica, &c. So numerous did the Dutch scholars become in Yedo that there arose two Dutch schools, the Down-town and the Up-town—the latter devoting its attention to the study of western history, politics, military and naval tactics, the former to that of medicine and kindred

---

[1] A very significant story is told of the celebrated Prince of Mito, a grandson of Iyeyasu. Among his retainers was a Christian believer, who was well-known for his loyalty and bravery. He made no secret of his faith and used to carry a banner with a cross on it. The prince summoned him to his presence and asked him the "reason of the hope that was in him." In answer thereto, the man held out a Chinese Testament, adding that his whole hope was to be found therein. Mito read and reread it with increasing interest. Finally he shut the book and wrote on its cover. "Surely this is a wonderful book, worthy of acceptance. Its effect is to create in the believer a longing for liberty and freedom, for which the present state of our country is not yet ripe." He sealed the book and wrote upon it. "Mito Komon forbids this book to be opened." It might greatly be doubted whether it was the dissemination of liberal principles that actuated our despotic rulers to shut out foreigners. If so, why did they admit the Dutch and the English, whose governments were respectively republican and constitutional, and exclude the Portuguese and the Spanish?

sciences. The Up-town party was led by Noboru Watanabe and Choei Takano, of whom we shall hear more presently. The law which was passed soon after the revolt of Shimabara, forbidding the acquisition of foreign languages and the possession of alien books, has been narrowed in its interpretation, since 1720, to religious works exclusively. The study of Dutch was pursued with impunity and became a favorite accomplishment among progressive youths.

About 1838 a rumor became current of the expected arrival of an English ship, the "Morrison," so named after the first English missionary to China. Her approach was communicated by the Dutch. The government suspected that she was coming to urge a commercial treaty at the muzzle of the cannon; hence forts were repaired and a few cannon cast. To Watanabe and Takano, to whom the character of the English navy was more or less familiar, such defensive preparations were ridiculous indeed. Takano published a pamphlet entitled "Story of a Dream," in which he laughed at the idea of firing at the English navy, and exposed what he deemed the silliest ignorance on the part of the government; that is taking *Morrison* for the name of a ship—"whereas," he says, "it is the name of an Englishman celebrated for his learning and long residence in China. Mr. Morrison," he continued, "has translated several Chinese works. If such an honorable personage should visit our country, the proper way would be to receive him with due respect and hospitality." It is not easy to determine how the name of *Morrison*[1] did become associated

---

[1] No English vessel or captain of this name came near the Japanese coast about this time. The nearest approach which we can find to this name is Matheson, the commander of a mariner: but he did not come (at least publicly) until 1849. Evidently Takano was thinking of Rev. Dr. Robert Morrison. If he did, he was himself mistaken in his strictures, for Dr. Morrison had been dead since 1834. Robert John Morrison, the son of the above, was living, but was not such a renowned personage as Takano described. The year previous to Takano's publication (*i. e.*, in 1837) an American ship of the name of *Morrison* had come to Uraga and also to Sat-

with the rumor; but whatever might be the Morrison gossip, Takano could not escape the fatal effect of his "Dream." Sentenced to perpetual imprisonment, he afterward escaped, and, changing his name and personal appearance, was secretly settled in his profession as a Dutch translator. The detectives were ever at his heels and he eluded an ignominious death only by falling by his own sword. His colleague, Watanabe, the author of a little miscellany, treating of the geography, physics, politics, &c., of European countries, was also put in jail; but he was subsequently released and confined to his country-home under bail. Seeing that his life was circumscribed in its sphere of work, and was a source of constant anxiety and care to his family and friends, he put an end to himself.

While Takano was secreting himself after his escape from custody and when Watanabe had been dead a year, another pioneer of western civilization appeared upon the stage, in the person of Shozan Sakuma. He was more conspicuous than his predecessors, on account of the European costume he adopted even in that early day. Well informed in European military tactics and histories, Shozan Sakuma addressed a letter to his feudal lord, in which, after dwelling upon the Chinese disasters of the Opium War and the growing power of Great Britain, he recommended eight measures as the best and only means of not sharing the fate of our Asiatic neighbor. The measures were: *firstly*, to construct forts in exposed places and to provide them with sufficient ammunition; *secondly*, to interdict the sale of copper to the Dutch, but use it in the manufacture of cannon; *thirdly*, to build ships after the western model, to be used in transporting provisions to Yedo in case of need; *fourthly*, to organize an admiralty, to encourage navigation and navy; *fifthly*, to build men-of-war, modeled

---

sums of which a full account is given in Chap. II. As she did not stay any length of time in our waters, nor touch the land, very likely her name was not known at the time of her arrival and the popular expectation of the *Morrison* was likely to have been a mistaken report of the belated news.

after the western pattern, and train mariners for emergency; *sixthly*, to establish schools even in the smallest villages, to instruct the people in the principles of morals; *seventhly*, to observe strict justice in rewarding merit or punishing crime, so that people may feel respect for the law and gratitude to authority; *eighthly* and lastly, to institute a general representation of feudal principalities. Sakuma emphasized the first measure, and, citing the life and work of Peter the Great, urged the Prince to carry his advice into practice. "Let the English," says he, "only know that we are ready to hurl them back; then they dare not come. The noblest of conquests is that won without bloodshed." He says, elsewhere, "The ancestral policy of self-contentment must be done away with. If it was adopted by your forefathers, because it was wise in their time, why not adopt a new policy if it is sure to prove wise in your time?" This memorial was written in 1841, twelve years before the advent of the American, Perry.

Sakuma fell a victim (Aug. 12, 1864,) to an assassin's dagger, but his principles survived his life. The decade between 1841-51 saw some ships built upon a Dutch model, arsenals, gun-foundries, docks and forts established, the assembly of territorial representations called into existence, several schools organized. Thus eleven years rolled on with much anxiety on the part of the rulers and plenty of work on the part of the populace. The dock-yards and the factories still resounded with the song of the Black Ship. Rightly to understand how the predictions of the ballad were realized, we must be aware of another important fact, or rather factor, in the recent progress of Japan. Let us therefore briefly consider

The Political State of Japan in the Middle of the Century.

Japan has been a monarchy since the beginning of the nation in 660 B. C.,[1] and the same dynasty has been ruling

---

[1] This date is not satisfactorily settled among historians. See Wm. Bramsen, *Japanese Chronological Tables*, p. 32, who is inclined to fix the accession of Jimmu at 130 B. C.

the country ever since without interruption. Owing to various causes which it is not necessary to enumerate here, the germ of the dual government was sown in the seventh century A. D. Watered by incessant wars, the plant grew in the twelfth century to bear the gaudy flower of the Shogunate (Generalissimoship), at the expense of the Imperial vitality, which soon dwindled into nominal sovereignty. Hence, in reading the history of Japan from the end of the twelfth century to the middle of this, it must ever be borne in mind that there existed an authority transcending, so to speak, the subordinate but *de facto* more powerful authority of the Shogun.[1] The Imperial Court was in Kyoto, the Shogun's capital shifted from place to place according as one family or another usurped the power. Since the domination of the Tokugawa house, it has been fixed at Yedo. The authority of the Shogun was acquired and preserved by military ascendency and artful policy. For centuries it was not disputed, and peace was secured by suppression and oppression. But, as Carlyle preaches again and again, "A lie cannot last forever." About the end of the seventeenth century, under the auspices of the Prince of Mito (1622–1700), a voluminous history of Japan was published. It was completed in 1715. This was pre-eminently a history in the sense of Mr. Freeman's definition,—namely, "past politics." The burden of this ponderous work was Imperialism, and it cast a doubt upon the validity of the Shogunal power. It was not long before the doubt grew into

---

[1] To this the name of the dual government has been applied, but it was something entirely different from the so-called dual government of Sparta. Neither must it be thought that Kyoto was a Rome and Yedo an Aix-la-chapelle. Religious considerations had nothing to do with the question. Perhaps the nearest approach in European history to the growth of the Shogunate, is that of the Mayoralty of the Palace of Neustria and Austrasia; or the functional difference between the Mikado and the Shogun was, as Mr. Mossman suggests, like that between the Queen as the hereditary monarch, and the Duke of Cambridge as commander-in-chief of the forces.

denial. In 1827, Sanyo Rai brought to the public his "History of Japan," which, on account of its attractive style and convenient size, circulated everywhere and was everywhere read. The spirit which permeated this work was reverence for the Imperial throne; and the yearning which it manifested for its restoration, contributed not a little to undermine the Shogunate.

The revival of Chinese classics consequent upon the migration of the Chinese savants in the seventeenth and eighteenth centuries, reminded anew the scholars of Japan that they owed allegiance solely and singly to the Tenno (Emperor). The simultaneous revival of pure Shintoism,[1] which inculcated the divine right and descent of the Emperor, also conveyed the same political evangel.

The clash of the Imperial and Shogunal powers was inevitable, on either side of which the great principalities must take part. A gigantic thunder-storm clouded the political horizon. The whole country was to be split and the blood of brothers spilt. Had there not been a foreign foe—who proved to be a friend after all—at our gate, the intestine struggles would have been much severer. It was twenty-six years after Sanyo's History had seen the light that the Shogun, without the imperial consent, began the negotiations of a treaty with the United States. Those loyalists who had been gnashing their teeth at his audacity, found in this high-handed proceeding a pretext for censure. The comic song of the Black Ship died away, and in its place was heard the murmur of "Son-ô, Jô-i" (Reverence to the Emperor, Expulsion of foreigners), which soon swelled into a battle-cry and the roar of cannon.

---

[1] See an exceedingly well prepared study of the revival of *Pure Shinto*, by E. M. Satow in the appendix to Vol. III, of *Trans. of Asiatic Soc. of Jap.*

CHAPTER II.

COMMODORE PERRY AND HIS AMERICAN PREDECESSORS.

Early American Attempts at Negotiation.

During the last five years of the past century, Holland was under Napoleon, and her possessions and monopolies in the East were alike exposed to the English navy. To escape capture by English cruisers in the Indian seas, the Dutch in Batavia hired an American ship, the *Eliza* of New York, Captain Stewart.[1] In 1797, when Perry was but three years old, his predecessor, Captain Stewart, made a voyage to Nagasaki. This is the first American ship recorded as entering Japanese waters. Stewart's visits were repeated; but his conduct in connection with the wreck of the *Eliza*, which took place in 1798, having been suspected, he left the service of the East India Company, and in 1803 made his last voyage to Nagasaki from Bengal — this time independently of the Dutch. He asked for trade, which was of course refused.

Mention is made of a similar undertaking about the same time. In 1798, under the Dutch colors, James Devereux,[2] captain of an American ship—the *Franklin*—made his way to Japan. The next year a Salem vessel, under command of Captain John Derby, made a like voyage, also under charter of the East India Company.

Commodore Porter, who had been dispatched to the Pacific for the protection of American whalers from the depredations

---

[1] Doeff, quoted in *Manners and Customs of the Japanese*, Lond., 1852.
[2] This information came to my knowledge through the kindness of a fellow student at the Johns Hopkins University, Mr. Langdon Williams, a great-grandson of Captain Stewart. The particulars of the voyage are to be found in the *Historical Collections of the Essex Institute*, Vol. II, p. 207, No. 6, Dec., 1860.

of British rivalry, addressed a letter in 1815 to Secretary Monroe, on the subject of opening Japan. In consequence of this, it was intended to send out the Commodore with a frigate and two sloops of war; but the plan was defeated.[1]

A few years later the interest in Japan was again renewed by John Quincy Adams, who urged that it was the duty of Christian nations to open Japan and of Japan to respond, on the ground that no nation had a right to withdraw its private contribution to the welfare of the whole human race.[2]

The first official attempt to establish commercial relations, was to have been made in 1832, when Edmund Roberts was appointed a special agent to negotiate treaties with oriental nations. Death came too soon for his mission (1836).[3] About this time, a separate expedition to Japan was also under contemplation by the United States government.

Five years later the merchantman *Morrison*, which has already been alluded to, was equipped by an American house, King & Co., in Macao. The object was an errand of mercy. To avoid suspicion, guns and armament were left behind. The ship carried, besides several presents, three souls who did much for the cause of religion and civilization,—namely, Drs. Peter Parker, Charles Gutzlaff and S. Wells Williams.[4] Of these, the last had learned the Japanese language from the shipwrecked Japanese who remained for some time in China, and whom it was the mission of the party to return home. The *Morrison*, in spite of her motive, was fired upon as she entered the Bay of Yedo, July 29, 1837. She weighed anchor and ran for the Kagoshima Bay, where she met the same

---

[1] De Bow's *Review*, Vol. XIII, 560.
[2] See *North American Rev.*, LXXXIII, 258.
[3] See Embassy to the Eastern Courts, mentioned in Griffis' *Perry*, 273.
[4] Dr. Williams sums up the result of this voyage: "Commercially speaking, the voyage cost about $2,000 without any return; and the immediate effects in a missionary or scientific way, were nil. But not finally. The seven men brought back were employed in one way or another, and most of them usefully." *Life and Letters of S. W. Williams*, by his Son, N. Y., 1889, p. 99.

reception, and then left the country without landing even the poor natives.

Mr. King falls into meditation at the result of his philanthropic enterprise and asks: "Why is the sentence of exclusion passed upon the Spaniards and Portuguese of 1637 entailed upon us, the descendants of those western colonists at the distance of two centuries?"[1] In strongest terms, he appeals to Christian sympathies and commercial interests and to the republican glories of America, for the opening of Japan.

In 1845, three Japanese fishermen who had been blown all the way from their native land to one of the Micronesian Islands, were carried by the frigate, St. *Louis*, to Ningpo in China, whence they were to be sent home.[2] One of them objected to being returned to his country, where the law required any citizen who had been abroad to be put to death, and the proposal was abandoned.

The *Manhattan* of Sag Harbor, Captain M. Cooper, carried eleven (some say 22) castaways from St. Peter's, in April of the same year, but she met with no better reception than the *Morrison*.

It was also early in 1845 that the Hon. Zadoc Pratt (Prattsville, Green Co., N. Y.), member of Congress and chairman of the select committee on statistics, laid before the House a report concerning the advisability of taking prompt action by sending an embassy to Japan and Korea.[3]

The interest in Japan did not end with the year, for, in the summer of the next year,

Commodore Bickle

led an expedition with a fleet consisting of the *Columbus* and the *Vincennes*. He carried a friendly letter from President

---

[1] *The voyage of the Morrison*, p. 173.
[2] Davis, *China*, Vol. II, p. 266.
[3] For particulars, see Lanman, *Leading Men of Japan*, p. 399. Cf. Ex. Doc., Vol. III, No. 138, 2d Session, 29th Cong.

Polk to the Emperor. The special object of the expedition was to ascertain whether the ports of Japan were accessible. The Commodore, after a stay of ten days in the Bay of Yedo, departed upon the receipt of the following anonymous explanatory edict:[1]

"The object of this communication is to explain the reasons why we refuse to trade with foreigners who come to this country across the ocean for that purpose.

"This has been the habit of our nation from time immemorial. In all cases of a similar kind that have occurred, we have positively refused to trade. Foreigners have come to us from various quarters, but have always been received in the same way. In taking this course with regard to you, we only pursue our accustomed policy. We can make no distinction between different foreign nations—we treat them all alike; and you, as Americans, must receive the same answer with the rest. It will be of no use to renew the attempt, as all applications of the kind, however numerous they may be, will be steadily rejected.

"We are aware that our customs are in this respect different from those of some other countries, but every nation has a right to manage its affairs in its own way.

"The trade carried on with the Dutch at Nagasaki, is not to be regarded as furnishing a precedent for trade with other foreign nations. The place is one of few inhabitants and very little business, and the whole affair is of no importance.

"In conclusion, we have to say that the Emperor positively refuses the permission you desire. He earnestly advises you to depart immediately, and to consult your own safety by not appearing again upon our coast."

Such was the defiant expression of the exclusive policy in its dying hours. If one sees therein gross barbarism, does he not withal note a consciousness of strength and independence,

---

[1] Cf. *Senate Doc.*, 1st session, 32d Cong., Vol. IX. The edict bears neither signature, nor date, nor address. It might have been written by an irresponsible person to meet urgent demands.

in striking contrast to the present slavish admiration of everything western, in which, in the name of science and reason, so many of our people freely indulge?

Wrecks of Whalers.

The same year, but about two months earlier (May, 1846) than the advent of Commodore Biddle, the *Lawrence*—Captain Baker—which had sailed from Poughkeepsie the previous summer on a whaling voyage, was wrecked on the coast of a Kurile Island. Seven of the crew survived and landed on the coast, where they were kindly treated by the people, but were soon discovered by officers and thrown into prison. One escaped, but in the excitement which attended his recapture he was killed. "At last," says one of them, "after seventeen months in all, of close and strict confinement, privation and ill-treatment, we were liberated and sent to Batavia by a Dutch vessel."

Two years later, the crew of another whaler, the *Ladoga*,[1] on account of bad treatment, deserted the ship in five boats, two of which were soon swamped. The surviving three parties, consisting of fifteen men—nine of whom were Sandwich Islanders—drifted upon an islet near the town of Matsumai (now Fukushima). Under a suspicion that they were spies, they were put in jail in Matsumai and afterward in Nagasaki. Their repeated attempts to break away from the prison only seemed to confirm the Japanese in their suspicion, and the rigors of confinement were doubled. One Maury, a Hawaiian, hung himself in the prison; Ezra Goldthwait died of a disease, or, as was charged, of a medicine prescribed by a quack. Suffering under brutal treatment one day, "on being taken out of our stocks," so narrates one of the prisoners, "we told the Japanese guards that their cruelty to us would

---

[1] For interesting particulars, see *Senate Doc.*, 1st Session, 32d Congress, Vol. IX.

be told the Americans, who would come here and take vengeance on them. Our guards replied, sneeringly, that they knew better, and that the Americans did not care how poor sailors were treated; if they did, then they should have come and punished the Japanese at Yedo, when a Japanese had insulted an American chief."

The circumstance referred to occurred at the interview of Com. Biddle with Japanese officers. To put it in the words of the Commodore himself, "I went alongside the junk in the ship's boat, in my uniform; at the moment that I was stepping on board, a Japanese on the deck of the junk gave me a blow or push, which threw me back into the boat." The conduct of the man was, as the Commodore himself said, inexplicable; but, with the assurance from the native officials that the man would be severely punished, the whole affair did not end in graver consequences.

With nothing to break the monotony of their irksome captivity, except growls and threats from the guards, the poor sailors of the *Ladoga* were on the verge of despair, when one evening a report of a distant gun, a sure signal of the approach of a foreign ship, reached their ears. A foreign ship it was. James Glynn, Commander of the U. S. ship *Preble*, was dispatched by Commodore D. Geisinger upon the advice of John W. Davis, U. S. Commissioner to China, to whom the news of the captivity of the *Ladoga's* crew was communicated from J. H. Levyssohn, Superintendent of the Dutch trade in Deshima. The *Preble* entered the harbor of Nagasaki on the 17th of April, 1849. After a week's conference, it was arranged that the ship-wrecked mariners who had been suffering so long from the effect of their misfortune, should be delivered up immediately. Accordingly, on the 26th, they were all carried to the town-house, where, for the first time, they unexpectedly met another of their countrymen, McDonald, who had been lodged in another part of the town. They were all taken away by Commander Glynn.

A Curious Youth.

The story of the above mentioned Ronald McDonald is so unique as to be worthy of further notice. Born in Astoria, Oregon, he had probably heard in his childhood the country of Japan frequently mentioned, or had in all likelihood seen the Japanese who were drifted ashore at the mouth of the Columbia River, in 1831. In 1845, when in his twenties, he shipped at Sag Harbor in a whale ship, the *Plymouth*. He made an arrangement with the captain that when they neared the coast of Japan, he should be left alone in a small boat, so contrived that he could capsize it himself. It was his intention to cast himself ashore and obtain some knowledge of the land and the people of this *terra incognita*. He was accordingly set adrift, and coasted along the shore for a day or two, when he discerned some fishermen at a distance. He beckoned to them, and, as they approached, he jumped into their boat and landed with them about twenty-five miles from Soya in Hokkaido. During the eight days that he remained under the roof of the fishermen, he was most kindly treated; but the good people, fearing that they were disloyal to the law in harboring a foreigner, notified an officer of his presence, and when he came poor McDonald was taken to Matsumai and afterwards transferred to Nagasaki. In each of these places he was well attended to. Lodging was provided him in a temple, and, though narrowly watched, he was not treated like a prisoner; but was allowed to occupy himself in teaching English. Whatever the young man's motive might have been in coming to Japan, in his work, although it is little noticed and less known, we trace a promise of American educational activity in Japan.

Service of the Whale in American-Japanese Intercourse.

The very year (1848) that the crew of the *Ladoga* were wrecked and McDonald of the *Plymouth* succeeded in landing (both of these ships were on whaling voyages), three American sailors belonging to another whaler—the *Trident*—were wrecked on one of the Kurile Islands. They, together with some twenty-seven English seamen who were wrecked also while out whaling, were returned home through the Dutch factory.

It is estimated that about the middle of the present century, American capital to the amount of seventeen million dollars was invested in the whaling industry in the seas of Japan and China.[1] We thus see that it was not a mere outburst of French enthusiasm when M. Michelet paid this high tribute to the service of the whale to civilization:[2] "Who opened to men the great distant navigation? Who revealed the ocean and marked out its zones and its liquid highways? Who discovered the secrets of the globe? The Whale and the Whaler. . . . . It was the whale that emancipated fishermen and led them afar. It led them onward and onward still, until they found it, after having almost unconsciously passed from one world to the other."

That the narrow cleft in the sealed door of Japan, into which Perry drove his wedge of diplomacy, was the rescue of American whalers, Mr. Fillmore implies in his address before the club of the Buffalo Historical Society: "The proceedings which resulted in the opening of Japan, sprang from a wrong perpetrated by that nation and which, like many other wrongs, seems to have resulted in a great good."[3]

Causes of the Expedition.

There were causes other than the mere safety of whalers which led to the inception of the American expedition to Japan. On the one hand, the rise of industrial and commer-

---

[1] Griffis, *Perry*, 296.
[2] Of the direct and indirect effects of whale fishing in the national development of Great Britain and of the United States, see Alexander Starbuck, *History of American Whale Fishery*, pp. 3, 97. *Propagation of Food Fishes*, 1875–6. *Mis. Senate Doc.*
[3] *American Historical Records*, Vol. III, 148.

cial commonwealths on the Pacific,[1] the discovery of gold in California, the increasing trade with China, the development of steam navigation—necessitating coal depots and ports for shelter,[2] the opening of highways across the Isthmus[3] of Central America, the missionary enterprise on the Asiatic continent, the rise of the Hawaiian Islands,—on the other hand, the knowledge of foreign nations among the ruling class in Japan, the news of the British victory in China, the progress of European settlements in the Pacific, the dissemination of western science among a progressive class of scholars, the advice from the Dutch government to discontinue the antiquated policy of exclusion—all these testified that the fulness of time for Japan to turn a new page in her history was at hand.

We have elsewhere considered some of the personages who, at different times, called the attention of the public and the government to the advantages to be derived from sending expeditions to Japan. Here let us consider a few others with whom the Perry Expedition is more immediately connected. The honor of the inception of the expedition has been claimed by several; but, much as we would do "honor to whom honor is due," history is by far the best judge, and history in this case distributes the meed of honor to many, according to their merits. To one (Aaron H. Palmer) is awarded the prize for his tireless industry in concentrating all the light he could upon the obscure shut-up country. Another (Glynn) was serviceable in planning a diplomatic scheme. The third

---

[1] Cf. *Annual Report of the Sec. of the Navy*, 1852.
[2] From the Golden Gate to Shanghai it is 6475 sea miles. To sail this distance, the sailing ships must have harbors where they could get provisions and fresh water, the steamers must have depots at which to load coal. The only place where they could do this, was the Sandwich Islands—2098 miles from San Francisco. "Can we not find shelter and coal in Japan?" was only a natural question to the Americans.
[3] Von Humboldt said that "this neck of land has been for many ages the bulwark of the independence of China and Japan."

(Webster) brought the weight of his official position to bear upon the plan of expedition. But—as for the inception—it was an old story, and no politician or warrior should reap that honor for himself alone. Rather let the humble American whalers — groaning in Japanese prisons — be crowned with the laurels for which the great and the boisterous clamor. For where could the idea of the necessity of sending an expedition begin more aptly, or come with greater force than in those dark dungeons, damp and drear, where lay "the poor white men" longing for home and heaven?

Just before the Expedition,

in the year 1848, Robert J. Walker, then Secretary of the Treasury, called public attention to "Japan, highly advanced in civilization, containing fifty millions of people, separated but two weeks by steam from our western coast. . . . Its commerce," he continues, "can be secured to us by persevering and peaceful efforts."[1]

During the next year, Aaron Haight Palmer of New York, who accumulated what was at that time a vast amount of information as to oriental nations, in his capacity as Director of the American and Foreign Agency of New York (1830-'47), saw the great necessity of establishing commercial relations with the East, and sent memorials upon the subject to the President and the Secretary of State. He was backed by memorials from the principal merchants of New York and Baltimore. In his letter[2] to Secretary Clayton, on the plan of opening Japan, he recommends four measures to be followed: (1) to demand full and ample indemnity for the shipwrecked American seamen who were unjustly treated; (2) to insist upon the proper care for any American who might from any misfor-

---

[1] *Reports on the Finances*, 1846-1849, p. 294.
[2] Cf. Palmer, *Origin of the Mission to Japan*, pp. 12, 13. Extracts from his writings on Japan are to be found in many newspapers of the times.

tune repair to the coast of Japan; (3) to enforce the opening of ports for commerce and for the establishment of consulates; (4) to claim the privilege of establishing coaling stations, and also the right of whaling without molestation. Mr. Palmer says that, in the event of non-compliance with the above on the part of the Shogun, a strict blockade of the Yedo Bay should be established.

James Glynn, who had for two years been cruising about the North Pacific Ocean, and who, as we have seen, had opportunities to learn something of the Japanese people, writing[1] in 1851 of the prospect of Chinese trade, speaks of the absolute necessity for a coal depot on the coast of Japan; and in his letter expresses a strong belief in the possibility of securing such a depot by proper negotiation, and eventually opening the whole Empire.

About this time, a newspaper article concerning some Japanese waifs who had been picked up at sea by the barque *Auckland*—Captain Jennings—and brought to San Francisco, attracted the attention of Commodore Aulick.[2] He submitted a proposal to the government that it should take advantage of this incident to open commercial relations with the Empire, or at least to manifest the friendly feelings of the country. This proposal was made on the 9th of May, 1851. Daniel Webster was then Secretary of State, and in him Aulick found a ready friend. The opinions of Commander Glynn and Mr. Palmer were asked, as being authorities on questions connected with Japan. Their letters on this occasion evince keen diplomatic sagacity.

Clothed with full power to negotiate and sign treaties, and furnished with a letter[3] from President Fillmore to the Em-

---

[1] The letter is addressed to Messrs. Howland and Aspinwall, Feb. 24, 1851.

[2] A gentleman attempts to prove that with Aulick began the idea of sending a Japanese expedition. Cf. *Publications of the Maryland Hist. Soc.*, Vol. III.

[3] The original of this letter was drafted by Webster himself. The letter which Perry took with him was in the main identical with this, though slightly changed by Everett.

peror, Commodore Aulick was on the eve of departure when for some reason[1] he was prevented. Thus the project which began at his suggestion was obstructed when it was about to be accomplished, and another man, perhaps better fitted for the undertaking, entered into his labors.

Sketch of Perry's Life.

Commodore Perry was descended from Edward Perry, a preacher of the Society of Friends, who settled in Plymouth in the latter half of the seventeenth century. The strong combative character of the family, of which Edward Perry's more illustrious posterity have given ample illustrations, is exhibited in this peace-man, who displeased the court not a little by writing against its abuses. He left Plymouth and with Roger Williams went to Rhode Island, where he spent the rest of his life. An account given of the Commodore's father shows that the family had abandoned Quaker views. We see him in the Revolutionary War captured and taken to Ireland. In this country he found his wife, and the four sons who were the fruit of this marriage were all distinguished for their naval achievements, one being especially conspicuous in American history for his naval manœuvres in Lake Erie.

Matthew Calbraith Perry was born in Newport, R. I., on the 10th of April, 1794. At the age of fifteen he was appointed a midshipman, and four years later was made a lieutenant. In 1819 he was engaged in founding a colony in Liberia, and a few years later he cruised in the West Indies capturing pirates. For some time he filled the post of the superintendent of a school for gun practice. Later he coöperated in the siege of Vera Cruz. In each of these positions he proved himself a man of sterling character and of great executive capacity.

---

[1] Some state that it was on account of his improper conduct to a South American Minister, whom he took home under his charge. Mr. Palmer says he fell ill. Griffis speaks of an unhappy mistake. Compare Griffis' Perry, pp. 284–289.

In certain circles of American society, the question of opening Japan was a favorite topic of discussion about the middle of this century. Commodore Perry shared the belief in the expediency of sending a special mission for the purpose. When Commodore Aulick was recalled, Perry proposed to the U. S. Government an immediate expedition. The proposal was accepted, and an expedition on the most liberal scale was resolved upon. He was invested with extraordinary powers, naval and diplomatic. The East India and China Seas and Japan were the official designation of the field of service, but the real object in view was the establishment of a coal depot in Japan. The public announcement of the resolution was followed by applications from all quarters of Christendom for permission to accompany the expedition; all these were, however, refused on prudential grounds.

What the World said of the Expedition.

The press, the mouthpiece of public sentiment, both in America and Europe, was free and fruitful in its comments on the intended expedition. A Washington correspondent of a Philadelphia paper writes that there " is no money (a constant excuse and always an efficacious one, too,) in the treasury for the conquest of the Japanese Empire, and that the administration will hardly be disposed to pursue such a romantic notion.[1] A correspondent to the Baltimore Sun,[2] in Washington, only two days before the expedition sailed, confidently remarks that " it will sail about the same time with Rufus Porter's aërial ship;" and after it sailed[3] insists on "abandoning this humbug, for it has become a matter of ridicule abroad and at home."

Not the less sarcastic are the English comments. The Times, quoted in Griffis' Perry, 308, doubts "whether the Emperor of Japan would receive Commodore Perry with most

---

[1] The Public Ledger, Nov. 18, 1853.
[2] Nov. 22, 1852.
[3] Baltimore Sun, Nov. 25, 1852.

indignation or most contempt," and *Punch* insisted that "Perry must open the Japanese ports, even if he has to open his own." "For ourselves," says the *London Sun*,[1] "we look forward to that result with some such interest as we might suppose would be awakened among the generality, were a balloon to soar off to one of the planets under the direction of some experienced aëronaut." Another London contemporary[2] "cannot agree with an American journalist in thinking such a force (2,000 men) will be sufficient to coerce a vain, ignorant, semi-barbarous and sanguinary nation of thirty millions of people." The *Dublin Nation* has also something to say on the benefits of the march of civilization into the darkness of heathendom, and reflects with pious horror and pity on the cruelties which "disgrace the British name in India," and the apocryphal conversions achieved in Southern Africa.[3]

Many other comments to the same effect, on the issue of the expedition, might be quoted if space allowed. If all these are but expressions of frail mortals, with whom to err is human, let us reverently listen to the solemn words of the prophet "Zadkiel." In his Almanac[4] occurs the following:

"A total eclipse of the Sun, visible chiefly in the eastern and northern parts of Asia. The greatest eclipse at 3 h. 24 m. A. M., December 11th, Greenwich time. . . . . . It will produce great mortality among camels and horses in the East, also much fighting and warlike doings, and I judge that it will carry war into the peaceful vales of Japan, for there, too, do the men of the West follow the track of gain, 'seeking the bubble reputation, even in the cannon's mouth.'"

No less a personage than the Earl of Ellesmere confessed, in 1855, that a few years previous he "saw little prospect of relaxation in the Japanese code of rigid exclusion without the employment of actual force."[5]

---
[1] Oct. 19, 1852.
[2] *London Examiner*, April 17, 1852.
[3] April 13, 1852.
[4] London, 1852, p. 39.
[5] See his inaugural address as President, in the *Journal of London Geogr. Soc.*, 1855, Vol. XXV, cxiv.

Voyage of Perry's Squadron.

Impatient of the delay caused by the tardy preparations of his vessels, Perry sailed from Norfolk on the 24th of November, 1852, with one ship, the *Mississippi*, leaving the rest to follow as soon as ready. When he had been gone three weeks, he wrote from Madeira to the Secretary of the Navy, his own views on the best course to pursue in his diplomacy. He dwells upon the necessity of establishing places of rendezvous in the Loo-Choo Islands. Such a measure "strikes him as not only justified by the strictest rules of moral law, but, which is also to be considered, by the laws of stern necessity, and the argument may be further strengthened by the certain consequences of amelioration of the conditions of the natives." To prove the wisdom of his proposal, he brings in the weight of his experience on the coast of Africa and in the Gulf of Mexico, where "it fell to his lot to subjugate many towns and communities." The answer of the President to this communication was in direct contrast, inculcating the spirit of peace.

On sailed the *Mississippi*, and, touching at several ports on her way, reached Loo Choo in May, where the squadron united. Some time was here spent in explorations, the detailed account of which was enlivened by the pen of Bayard Taylor, who was of the party.

The next place at which they stopped was the Munin (Bonin) Islands. These lie in the 27th degree of north latitude, and were discovered in 1593 by a Japanese navigator. They were subsequently visited and occupied by people of different nationalities. The favorable situation of the islands suggested to Perry the plan of establishing an American colony there, which would serve quadruple purposes; namely, as a coal depot, a rendezvous, a resort of whaling vessels for refitment, and as a future missionary station. But soon weightier matters than the settlement of the Bonin Islands absorbed the attention of the Commodore. He returned to Napha, and early on the 2nd of July departed thence.

Let it be here mentioned that the charts used in the expedition came, according to Griffis,[1] mostly from Holland, and cost the U. S. Government some $30,000. The price of von Siebold's *Archiv* alone was $503. Admiral Sir G. Seymour, then in command of the Pacific, had also put into Perry's hands a large quantity of charts of the seas in question.[2]

The Squadron in Yedo Bay.

After a six days' voyage from Napha, in the afternoon of the 8th of July, 1853, the squadron entered the Bay of Yedo in martial order, and about 5 o'clock in the evening was anchored off the town of Uraga.

No sooner had "the black ships of the evil mien" made their entry into the Bay, than the signal guns were fired, followed by the discharge of rockets; then were seen on the shore companies of soldiers moving from garrison to garrison. The popular commotion in Yedo at the news of "a foreign invasion," was beyond description. The whole city was in an uproar. In all directions were seen mothers flying with children in their arms, and men with mothers on their backs. Rumors of an immediate action, exaggerated each time they were communicated from mouth to mouth, added horror to the horror-stricken. The tramp of war-horses, the clatter of armed warriors, the noise of carts, the parade of firemen, the incessant tolling of bells, the shrieks of women, the cries of children, dinning all the streets of a city of more than a million souls, made confusion worse confounded.

Not so badly alarmed were the Shogun's officials. They

---

[1] *Perry*, 294.
[2] Earl of Ellesmere's inaugural address. *Jour. of Lond. Geogr. Soc.*, Vol. XXV (1855), cxiv.

were not without a vague apprehension of this event. The Dutch had whispered about it some time before. Then, too, did not a verse of the founder of Yedo say:

"To my gate ships will come from the far East,
Ten thousand miles"?

They did not, however, show much composure in their deliberations. The hurried dispatches from the court of the Shogun to the *daimios*, summoning arms, commanding re-inforcement of forts, demanding contributions in money and implements of war, calling on priests to incur the favor of the gods, ordering this and that, made, indeed, "the night joint laborer with the day." This state of things continued for some days in Yedo.

As the squadron dropped anchor, it was surrounded by junks and boats of all sorts, but there was no hostile sign shown. A document in French was handed on board, which proved to be a warning to any foreign vessel not to come nearer.

The next day was spent in informal conference between the local officials of Uraga and the subordinate officers of the squadron. It was Commodore Perry's policy to behave with as much reserve and exclusiveness as the Japanese diplomats had done and would do. He would neither see, nor talk with, any except the highest dignitary of the realm. Meanwhile, the governor of Uraga came on board and was received by captains and lieutenants. He declared that the laws forbade any foreign communication to be held elsewhere than Nagasaki; but to Nagasaki the squadron would never go. The vexed governor would send to Yedo for further instructions, and the 12th was fixed as a day for another conference. Any exchange of thought was either in the Dutch language, for which interpreters were provided on both sides, or in Chinese, through Dr. S. Wells Williams, and afterward in Japanese, through Manjiro Nakahama.

The third day, the 10th, was Sunday. On shore there was no sign of peace on this day of rest. Armed for defence, the warriors were ready "to imitate the action of a tiger," when suddenly a gentle breeze wafted the sound of music from the fleet. They listened; it was not a bugle, a drum or a trumpet. It was so melodious and withal so soft, that for a time it dispelled their bloody passions and soothed their fiery hearts. Though history takes no cognizance of the tangible effect of this Christian service, though the time looks still afar off for the fulfilment of the hymn then sung,

> "Before Jehovah's awful throne,
> Ye nations, bow with sacred joy,"

let it be noticed as a sacred, moral fact in history.

On the 12th, the Governor of Uraga again appeared on board and insisted on the squadron's leaving the Yedo Bay for Nagasaki, where the President's letter would be duly received through the Dutch or the Chinese. This the Commodore firmly refused to do. It was therefore decided at the court of Yedo that the letter be received at Kurihama, a few miles from the town of Uraga. This procedure was, in the language of the commissioners, "in opposition to the Japanese law;" but, on the ground that "the Admiral, in his quality as Ambassador of the President, would be insulted by any other course," the original of Mr. Fillmore's letter to the Japanese Emperor, enclosed in a golden box of one thousand dollars in value, was delivered on the fourteenth of July to the commissioners appointed by the Shogun.

The Shogunate at its Wit's End.

The transaction had thus luckily ended without bloodshed, though at no small cost of time-honored pride, on the part of the Japanese. What next to do, was then the puzzle. The presence of an armed squadron so near the capital, the proud and daring conduct of the American officer, was not much to the Shogun's taste, if indeed to anybody's. Touch the temper of the foreign power by flat denial of any negotiation he dared

not. A definite negotiation of treaty would heap upon him the
anathema of the whole nation. Fortunately for Japan, the
disturbed state of affairs in China made it prudent for Perry to
repair to the ports of that country, which he did as though
he had consulted solely the diplomatic convenience of our
country. He left word that he would come the ensuing spring
for our answer.

Now the Bay is cleared of the obnoxious presence; the
President's letter is received; there are yet ten months to consider how to answer; meanwhile what shall we do? Let the
good will of the daimios be consulted, and the responsibility
of war or peace, as the case may prove, be shared by them.
Copies of President Fillmore's letter are therefore sent to all
the daimios and their unreserved opinions are requested.
Already on the 15th of July, before the circulars were sent
out, the Prince of Mito had sent in his memorial on the subject, which, as it shows the general tenor of

The Spirit of the Times,

is here inserted at some length. It says:

"There are ten reasons in favor of war (which means the
refusal of treaty).

"1st. The annals of our history speak of the exploits of
the great, who planted our banners on alien soil; but never
was the clash of foreign arms heard within the precincts of
our holy ground. Let not our generation be the first to see
the disgrace of a barbarian army treading on the land where
our fathers rest.

"2nd. Notwithstanding the strict interdiction of Christianity, there are those guilty of the heinous crime of professing the doctrines of this evil sect. If now America be once
admitted into our favor, the rise of this faith is a matter of
certainty.

"3rd. What! Trade our gold, silver, copper, iron and
sundry useful materials, for wool, glass and similar trashy

little articles. Even the limited barter of the Dutch factory ought to have been stopped.

"4th. Many a time, recently, have Russia and other countries solicited trade with us; but they were refused. If once America is permitted the privilege, what excuse is there for not extending the same to other nations?

"5th. The policy of the barbarians is first to enter a country for trade, then to introduce their religion and afterward to stir up strife and contention. Be guided by the experience of our forefathers two centuries back; despise not the teachings of the Chinese Opium War.

"6th. The 'Dutch scholars' say that our people should cross the ocean, go to other countries and engage in active trade. This is all very desirable, provided they be as brave and strong as were their ancestors in olden times; but, at present, the long continued peace has incapacitated them for any such activity.

"7th. The necessity of caution against the ships now lying in harbor (*i. e.* Perry's Squadron), has brought the valiant *samurai* to the capital from distant quarters. Is it wise to disappoint them?

"8th. Not only the naval defence of Nagasaki, but all things relating to foreign affairs, have been entrusted to the two clans of Kuroda and Nabeshima. To hold any conference with a foreign power, outside of the port of Nagasaki—as has been done this time at Uraga—is to encroach upon their rights and trust. These powerful families will not thankfully accept an intrusion into their vested authority.

"9th. The haughty demeanor of the barbarians now at anchorage, has provoked even the illiterate populace. Should nothing be done to show that the government shares the indignation of the people, they will lose all fear and respect for it.

"10th. Peace and prosperity of long duration have enervated the spirit, rusted the armor and blunted the swords of our men. Dulled to ease, when shall they be aroused? Is not the present the most auspicious moment to quicken their sinews of war?"

Three weeks after the above memorial had been drafted, there were some forty answers sent in by daimios and principal dignitaries of the State. Almost unanimously they declared against opening the country, whatever consequences might follow. Some of them would try the experiment of foreign commerce for three years, others five and still others ten, to test how such a novel scheme would work, and at the end of the period, by which time the national armament would be more or less complete, give a definite answer to the proposals of the United States government. So thought the Shogun's court, and that the people concurred in this, was shown by the popularity of a little book entitled "Coast Defence," in which the author harangued in most vehement terms the foreigners and the foreign trade. Meanwhile warlike preparations were briskly made. The forts of Shinagawa, which now so conspicuously dot the coast, were constructed at this time. Bells from monasteries, metal articles of luxury from opulent families, were cast into cannon and bombs. Patriots to the number of more than three hundred thousand, flocked to Yedo; a certain number repaired to Kyoto.

Perry had not been gone two months, when the Russian Admiral Pontiatine anchored in the Bay of Nagasaki and demanded three things of us: more neighborly intimacy, precision of the boundary-line in Saghalien and the opening of sea-ports. The English might also make their appearance at any time; for it was reported by the Dutch three years before, that the governor of India had obtained permission to negotiate a treaty with Japan. Nay, the British ships were already on Asiatic waters, to chase the Russians. In China, the Taiping Revolt was raging. In the midst of the rumors of war, died the Shogun. Thus, full of trials, the year of 1853 closed.

Perry's Second Visit and Treaty.

It was the Taiping Rebellion which called for Perry's presence in China. The American merchants had large interests at stake there—their property in Shanghai alone amounting, it is said, to $1,200,000.[1] The merchants, the governor of Shanghai and the U. S. agent, Mr. Marshall, all thought his presence required; but Perry thought otherwise. He advocated inactivity in the affair of the Rebellion.

While in China, Commodore Perry found that the Russian and French admirals who were staying in Shanghai, contemplated a near visit to Japan. That he might not give any advantage to them, he left Macao earlier than he had intended, and, on the 13th of February, found himself again in the Bay of Yedo, with a stately fleet of eight ships. As the place where the conference had been held at the previous visit, was out of the reach of gun-shot from the anchorage, Perry expressed a desire of holding negotiations in Yedo, a request impossible for the Japanese to comply with. After some hesitation, the suburb Kanagawa was mutually agreed upon as a suitable site, and there a temporary building was accordingly erected for the transaction of the business. On the 8th of May, Commodore Perry, arrayed in the paraphernalia befitting his rank, was ushered into the house.[2] The reply of the Shogun to the President's letter was now given—the purport of which was, decidedly in word but reluctantly in spirit, in favor of friendly intercourse. Conferences were repeated in the middle and latter part of the month, and after many evasions and equivocations, deliberations and delays, invitations to banquets and exchanges of presents, at last, on Friday, the 31st of May, the formal treaty was signed; a synopsis of which is here presented.

---

[1] Neumann, *Zeitschrift für allgemeine Erdkunde*, 1856, p. 324.

[2] In a number of the N. Y. Semi-weekly *Post*, published Jan. 1889 (see correspondence "Quaint Old Bladensburgh"), it is stated that "the first American flag ever used on the soil of Japan"—probably the flag used at this time—was left among the relics of Capt. Hunter in Cloudland Mansion, Bladensburgh, near Washington, D. C.

Synopsis of the treaty of Peace, Commerce and Navigation, Signed at Kanagawa 31st March, 1854.

I. Peace and friendship.
II. Ports of Shimoda and Hakodate open to American ships, and necessary provisions to be supplied them.
III. Relief to shipwrecked people; expenses thereof not to be refunded.
IV. Americans to be free as in other countries, but amenable to just laws.
V. Americans at Shimoda and Hakodate not to be subject to restrictions; free to go about within defined limits.
VI. Careful deliberation in transacting business which affects the welfare of either party.
VII. Trade in open ports subject to local regulations.
VIII. Wood, water, provisions, coal, etc., to be procured through Japanese officers only.
IX. Most-favored nation clause.
X. U. S. ships restricted to ports of Shimoda and Hakodate, except when forced by stress of weather.
XI. U. S. Consuls or agents to reside at Shimoda.
XII. Ratifications to be exchanged within eighteen months.

No sooner had the treaty been signed and exchanged than Commander H. A. Adams was dispatched to bear it home for ratification, which was promptly and unanimously made by the Senate. In the meantime, the harbors mentioned in the treaty were visited by American ships.

His labors at an end, Perry bade the last farewell to Japan and started on his home-bound voyage. This was in June, 1854. The next month he was in Hong Kong, where were awaiting him, from the Navy Department, replies to his request that he might return to the States as soon as his mission was accomplished. Delivering to Captain Abbott command of the squadron, with the best wishes and thanks of his countrymen in China for his services, he embarked in an English steamer.¹

Significance of the Treaty.

Thus did the sailor diplomat succeed in wresting from the reluctant nation a surety of friendship. Thus did Perry, America, Aryan civilization, science and Christianity triumph. Perry's—or let me say rather America's—coming was most providentially opportune. Had it been a little earlier, when the Japanese mind had not been prepared, or a little later when the whole country was plunged in intestine turmoil, there is no saying what might have been America's success or Japan's fate. Or had any other power than America—for instance Great Britain or France, whose strong policy in China had instilled dread and doubt into our people, or say Russia, whose movement in the North was more than suspicious—had any other power than America, in whom was no guile (at least so far as her dealings in the East were concerned, though what she did in Mexico was not entirely unknown to Japan even then), the course of Japanese history might have been very different from what it has been.

Still more providential than the point of time, was Perry's choice of the site of landing. Here he unconsciously displayed truest sagacity. As we have already seen, it was Perry's conviction that the isolation of Japan was not a result of national character, but merely of accidental policy; hence, to do away with it, he "must deal with the officials—the upholders and the tools of this exclusion system—as with his enemy; he must penetrate into the very seat of this evil, namely, into the

---

¹ Of Perry's life see Rev. Dr. Griffis' new book on the subject. Perry had his residence in Tarrytown, N. Y., where he was a neighbor to Washington Irving. He died on the 4th of March, 1858, and was buried in Newport, R. I., by the side of his mother's grave. Ten years later a bronze statue of heroic size, erected by Mr. Belmont of New York City, was unveiled in Touro Park, Newport.

court; he must confer with the highest officials."[1] If Perry had had better knowledge of the system of our duarchy, he would very likely have entered the Gulf of Osaka and knocked at the imperial gate of Kyoto for admission, and then—then civil wars would not have sufficed to make the New Japan. As he came into the Bay of Yedo and knocked at the portals of the Shogun, uncmaoked, though not without creaking, they opened on their rusty hinges. Thus two ends were gained by one effort:—the country was opened to foreign trade, and, at the same time, the abolition of feudalism and the Shogunate was hastened.

Services of the Dutch.

It is scarcely to be denied that the Dutch government, in the person of its representative, Donker Curtius, had taken a step before Perry's departure from the States, in persuading Japan of the follies and dangers of seclusion. It even went so far as to make a draft of a treaty, "based on the laws, customs and usages of Japan, which would attain the end in such a way as no other means can reach, and which, in case the Netherlands succeed, could confer the same advantages upon all other nations."[2] This proposed treaty, drawn up some time in the summer of 1852, was the outcome of the Dutch Cabinet orders of the 23d of March, and of the 9th of April of that year, to the general governor of the Dutch Indies. What induced these orders to be issued, was, in turn, the report of the preparations of the U. S. Expedition to Japan. In his letter dated November 2d, 1852, explaining the points of the proposed treaty, Donker Curtius writes to the governor of Nagasaki—"His Majesty, the King of the Netherlands, hopes and expects that peace will be granted Japan, should it answer the wishes of the U. S. President in this wise." A perusal of this proposed treaty, dwelling, as it does in many places, expressly

---

[1] Neumann, *Die Amerikanische Expedition nach Japan*, in *Zeitschrift für Allgemeine Erdkunde*, 1868, p. 319.

[2] See Bley, *Die Politik der Niederlande in ihren Beziehungen zu Japan*, 1885; also Siebold, *Eröffnung Japans*, p. 17.

or implicitly on the interests of the United States, clearly shows that Holland rendered that government a service.

It still remains to be seen how much Perry availed himself of this draft. The first article of Perry's treaty about peace and amity, is but a weaker repetition of Article I of the Netherland proposal, where the Dutch king assures Japan of his friendship, in case the latter should be implicated in war. Perry's demand (Article II) to have Shimoda and Matsumai as ports for the reception of American ships, is expressed in the Dutch treaty, Article IV, section 1, where two coaling stations are asked for,—the one in the north, in "the Bay of Good Hope," and the other in the south, on one of the islands of the Linschoten Archipelago. What Perry asks for, in Articles III and IV, respecting shipwrecked citizens of the United States, is found in substance in the Dutch Article II. In Article IV, though the point conceded is in the main the same as that implied in the Dutch Article VI, section b, still the former has included an express phrase to the effect that American citizens should not be confined and restricted as the Dutch and the Chinese in Nagasaki. In Article VI, Perry would have any business arrangement to be settled by "careful deliberation between the parties," and here he deprived the Shogunal government of the right to have everything its own way, as suggested by the Dutch Article IV, sections d, e and f; but, in Article VIII, Perry conceded that some articles should be obtained only "through the agency of Japanese officials appointed for the purpose." The most-favored nation clause, in Perry's Article IX,[1] is equivalent to Article VI of the Dutch treaty. Change the name of Nagasaki, in section a, Article IV of the Dutch treaty, to Shimoda and Hakodate, and we have Article VII of Perry's treaty. Perry's Article XI, in regard to the residence of United States consuls or agents in the treaty port, corresponds exactly to section b of the Dutch Article IV. The twelfth and last Article of

---

[1] This clause is said to have been inserted at Dr. Williams' suggestion. *Life and Letters*, 214.

Perry's treaty, about ratification, finds its parallel in the concluding article of the Dutch.

Thus considered and compared, one finds but little in Perry's treaty that is original. If it is an improvement that he introduced into Articles IV and V, an express demand for freedom for his countrymen, so can it be said, on the other hand, that he left out what Section j, Article IV, of the Dutch treaty requires; namely, extra-territorial rights.

The superiority of Perry's wisdom seems to lie not so much in single clauses of the treaty—not even so much in his diplomacy, as in the bold stroke of coming directly to Yedo, and, however much we may admire his personal skill, it is to this daring policy that we must in great measure attribute his success. Nor must we, in our just praise of his ability, forget that his squadron was the greatest that ever anchored so near the castle of Yedo.[1]

We speak now-a-days of the peaceful opening of our country as doing credit and honor to the Republic. We doubt, however, whether, until it became an accomplished fact, Perry was so peacefully inclined. In a letter to his government, written on his way to Japan, he by no means showed in his inclination the peaceful policy of his government. It is to the credit of the Republic that Perry was admonished not to resort to force. Siebold[2] gives an extract of a letter from his correspondent on board the *Mississippi*: "The object of the expedition is a difficult one and I fear that it will not be reached by peaceful means, though everything will be done to do it peacefully. But, in case force must be used, our expedition is strong enough to make a respectable impression. It consists of eight steamers and frigates with 230 cannon."

Legality of the Treaty.

Judging from the present results of the event, we see that what was, was right. Not so optimistic, however, did the

---

[1] Williams' *Life and Letters*, 194. [2] *Br Offnung Japans*, 18.

circumstances appear to the men of that age. When the Shogun's conclusion of the treaty was communicated to Kyoto, the royalists denounced it as treason and his dealings as fresh usurpations of imperial power. An impartial observer will find in the Shogun's proceeding no more assumption of power than the latitude which prestige allowed him. Iyeyasu apparently obtained no sanction from the Imperial Court, when he gave commercial privileges to the Dutch and the English in the sixteenth century. Neither did his descendants ask for it, when they issued edicts against Catholic missionaries. True, no formal treaty was contracted between the Dutch or the English and the Japanese. They never claimed trade with us as a right; rather did they look upon it as a favor, and as a favor did Iyeyasu on his part confer the privilege. The position of these foreigners was similar to that of the German merchants in the old Hanseatic Steelyards on the Thames. If King John, by giving permission to the traders of Bremen to start a factory in London, only exercised a royal prerogative of protection and hospitality to foreigners, Iyeyasu did likewise by the exercise of his Shogunal power, which was practically sovereign. If the Hanseatic factors considered themselves as guests on a friendly soil in London, so did the Dutch and the English in Nagasaki. If the "Easterlings," as the German merchants were called in England, maintained their foothold by New Year's donations to the Mayor and other dignitaries, so did the "Westerlings" in Japan hold theirs by their annual presents to the Shogun and his officials. If treaty-making power is an attribute of sovereignty, is not the generous bestowal of privileges to foreign subjects another?

The granting of commercial privileges by John and his successors to the "Easterlings," and of Iyeyasu and his descendants to the "Westerlings," only shows the wide latitude of power vested in the English monarch and tacitly endowed in the Shogun. As long as historical precedents alone are taken as a guide, in absence of a written constitution, the signing of Perry's treaty was an act of perfect legality on the part of the Shogun, and the Imperialists could find no

just cause of censure. But that they did find in it not only a
cause of complaint, but ultimately a reason for his deposition,
was due to the circumstances of the time, apart from this
special act of the Shogun. As has been described in a preceding chapter, the hour was ripe for the restoration of the
Imperial authority. Had the treaty been concluded when the
power of Yedo was at its former height, it is probable that no
questions would have been asked.

America Followed by Europe.

No sooner had Perry left, carrying off the trophy of peaceful
victory—the treaty (though the Yedo government was in no en-
joyment of peaceful rest), than the Russian Admiral Poutiatine
appeared in Nagasaki. He urged that the same privileges be
granted his country as were allowed the Americans. And how
can Japan refuse them to a *neighbor*? It is a convenient thing
to have a neighbor sometimes, though not always, for a neighbor
does not necessarily prove a good Samaritan!

Soon, the English Rear Admiral, Sir James Stirling, arrives
at the same harbor, very kindly to notify the government that
that there may be some fighting in Japanese waters between
Russians and his countrymen.

Tronson in his *Voyage to Japan*[1] (p. 20), gives an anecdote
which is suggestive: "A plain-spoken official said that he
understood that England was a very small country in the
western seas, strong by sea, and that the natives lived by
plundering the ships of peaceable nations and compelling all
to pay tribute. We took considerable (it must have been
considerable!) pains to enlighten our ignorant friend, etc.
. . . . . He remarked that all we said was very good, but
why go to war with Russia (a question worthy of John
Bright!), England and France against one power?" Whether
"our ignorant friend" was silenced with arguments or with
a show of what is falsely termed a "higher power," it is not

---

[1] The book gives a detailed account of the Admiral's visit.

known. The British convention was signed October 14, 1854, and followed, in 1858, by the Elgin treaty.

The treaty with Russia was signed January 26, 1855; Netherlands, 9th of November the same year; France, October 9, 1858; Portugal, 3rd of August, 1860; German Customs Union, 25th of January, 1861. The other nations which followed the United States were Italy, Spain, Denmark, Belgium, Switzerland, Austria-Hungary, Sweden and Norway, Peru, Hawaii, China, Corea and Siam; lastly Mexico, with whom we concluded a treaty on terms of *perfect equality* (Nov. 30, 1888).

Exchange of Ratifications.

We have seen Commander Adams dispatched to Washington, with tidings of the successful issue of the expedition. Early the next year (January, 1855), endowed with full powers as Representative of the United States, he came to Shimoda for the exchange of the ratifications. To this native authority interposed two technical objections: first, that according to the letter of the treaty it was to be ratified after eighteen months; secondly, that the Tycoon never signs any treaty. Without much difficulty these points were settled. The American draft of the treaty said *within* instead of *after* eighteen months. The other objection was done away with, by Commander Adams' explanation that the President and the Secretary of State had signed the instrument, and therefore must the corresponding personages in the Empire subscribe their signatures.

"On the day after the ratification, February 22," says Dr. Hawks in the closing paragraph of his "Narrative of the Japan Expedition," "the *Powhatan* (commanded by Adams) left Shimoda, and our new and, as we trust, enduring friendly relations with Japan are thus associated, in date at least, with the name of Washington."

A few weeks pass and we find the *Mississippi* moored in the Navy Yard at Brooklyn. There Commodore Perry repaired on board, and by formally hauling down his flag, brought to an auspicious close the United States Expedition to Japan.

CHAPTER III.

DIPLOMACY AND COMMERCE.

American Disappointment in Regard to Perry's Treaty.

In our considerations thus far, we have seen how the convention was concluded and between whom its ratifications were exchanged. It must have been observed that Perry's was not a commercial treaty; that the party with whom he negotiated was not the rightful Sovereign of the Empire. Great as was Perry's success, it was only a beginning. There were not a few of his countrymen who publicly asserted that his mission came very far short of their expectations. Mr. Hildreth[1] is unnecessarily severe in this respect. Daguerreotype views of the country were, in his opinion, to be the principal contribution made by Perry's expedition to western knowledge of Japan. Mr. Spalding[2] laughs at the parade and the assumed dignity of the Commodore while he was engaged in negotiation, and laughs, too, at the wild expectations of commercial men. The newspapers did not scruple to complain[3] because an immense trade was not immediately secured, and because Perry did not go the length of completing a commercial treaty. We can well sympathise with the disappointment of the American public, when we are told that the direct trade between the United States and Japan

---

[1] *Japan as it was and is*, Preface.
[2] *Japan Expedition*.
[3] See *North American Rev.*, Vol. 83, p. 264.

was originally (1852) estimated, at least, at 200,000,000 dollars annually to America.[1] But, after all, the opening of an obscure oriental country, but little talked of and less known, was to the every-day life of an American of little consequence. "The funeral of Bill Poole or the fillibustering operations in the Gulf of Mexico," says E. E. Hale,[2] "have (naturally) awakened more interest among the people, than has the opening, by peaceful diplomacy, of the Italy of the East to the intercourse of the world."

Japan soon after Perry's Departure.

Immediately after Perry's squadron had left the Japanese waters, the rulers of the country, whether actuated by clear foresight and comprehension of the moment, or whether impelled by that mental confusion which attends sudden awakening from slumber and apprehension of the next moment, were aroused to immediate activity. Schools were opened for the study of foreign languages; academies shot up, where youths could receive instruction in military and naval tactics; raw recruits were drilled; foundries and smithies sprang into existence, and belfries were molested to furnish metal for arsenals. To this last the bonzes objected; they would rather fight with the weapon of prayer, for, they asked: "Did not the prayers of the devout destroy the Armada of Kublai Khan?"

We who enjoy the blessings of New Japan, look back upon these times of our fathers, and thank Providence for the *peaceful* opening of our country; but peace there was none. Of peace of mind, why talk? Even peace of nature was disturbed. A succession of unusually severe earthquakes shook (1855) the southern provinces and also Yedo, throwing down a number of dwelling-houses, injuring and killing people by thousands.

---

[1] *De Bow's Review*, XIII, 561. See also T. Watts, *Japan and the Japanese*, 170.
[2] *North Amer. Review*, Vol. 83, p. 236.

In the midst of these catastrophes, was made public an announcement for which the people were in some measure prepared; that the Shogun had the previous year entered into treaty relations with America, England and Russia. Already there had come to Japan

American Pioneers of Commerce.

Only half a month after Perry had left, the clipper ship, *Lady Pierce*, with the owner, Silas E. Burrows, on board, arrived in Yedo Bay.[1] It was fitted out from San Francisco, with no other object than to boast of the honor of being the first trading vessel to enter the Japanese port. Mr. Burrows took with him a few shipwrecked Japanese. He returned with thanks and presents from the Japanese government.

Then came Messrs. Reed and Doty from Honolulu. They arrived at Shimoda three weeks after Commander Adams left.[2] Their destination was Hakodate, where it was their object to establish a supply depot for American whalers. They landed in Shimoda to pass the time until Hakodate should be opened; their families, including three women and some children, excited no small degree of curiosity among the natives. Here the merchants occupied themselves in purchasing lacquer-ware, rice, silks, etc., for San Francisco. It was not long before they were disturbed in their peaceful avocations, by a question as to their right of residence. This was the question mooted at the conference that immediately attended the signing of the treaty. American citizens could sojourn in Japanese ports, but their permanent residence was refused. The words of the commissioners then were: "We do not want any women to come and remain at Shimoda." Messrs. Reed and Doty were asked to leave the country as soon as they could. They sailed for Hakodate, but there again they were ordered away.

---

[1] Hildreth, *Japan as it was and is*, 584.
[2] Hawks, *Japan Expedition*, 463.

In August, 1855, an American schooner—the *Wilmington*—arrived at Shimoda from Hong Kong, with a cargo of miscellaneous articles. Not an article could be landed. Disappointed, she steered to Hakodate where she was no more successful.[1]

Advent of Townsend Harris.[2]

According to Article XI of the treaty, an American Consul-General, in the person of Townsend Harris, was sent to Shimoda in August, 1856. As a China-merchant in New York, Mr. Harris had devoted much attention to the interests of oriental commerce. He amassed a vast amount of knowledge by extensive travels as supercargo of his own ship, and had also spent some time in China. His appointment as Consul-General to Japan, in 1855, a year previous to his arrival at his post of duty, was therefore due to his familiarity with Eastern affairs. He was accompanied by one Mr. Heuskin, a native of Holland, as his clerk and interpreter. They spent the remainder of the year and the beginning of the next, in the little town of Shimoda, a large part of which had been destroyed by earthquake.

In the interim, the Council of Elders in Yedo received a memorandum from the Dutch, on the issue of the Opium War, on the siege of Sebastopol, on gold harvest in California, bread riots in Liverpool and sundry other bits of startling gossip from the outer world. The memorandum closed with a friendly, practical hint that Japan would better behave with greater diffidence and speak with more civility, in her intercourse with foreign nations. A word, a look in diplomacy, might be a source of lengthened woes! The hint was well received. Hence, when Townsend Harris urged upon the supreme

---

[1] *Commercial Relations*, 1856; Vol. I, p. 508.
[2] The writer is indebted to Judge Charles P. Daly, of New York City, for information regarding the life of Townsend Harris. The judge was an intimate friend of Mr. Harris.

authorities in Yedo the necessity of direct communication, the usage of two centuries and a half was set aside, in spite of public opinion, and the American representative was received at the court of the Shogun with the ceremony due his rank.¹ At this time, two young men conspired against his life, but they were arrested and shortly after died in prison. The wonder is that there were not many more of these would-be assassins. In fact, the anti-foreign feeling seems to have become dormant for a while. This was observed by Harris himself, who, during his illness in Yedo, was tenderly supplied with what he needed, by the Shoguness herself.

In a series of conferences held the next year (1857), Harris enlightened the Japanese novices in the science of diplomacy and the rudiments of International Law. He elucidated the different duties of a Minister and a Consul, the *modus operandi* of tariff legislation, and other points of similar nature. Harris was not content with lecturing on the doctrinal part of *jus gentium*, but, with that practical acumen which became a diplomat and an American, he concluded the conference with a vivid description of the war which was then ravaging China. The overbearing hauteur of the Celestials in their dealings with European nations—an obvious innuendo—was emphasised, as being a cause of the thousand and one evils that befell their country. Neither did he forget to intimate to the commissioners, that the British and French men-of-war were cruising in near waters.

In June of the same year, Minister Harris succeeded in concluding a convention, which, however, was only of an ephemeral nature, inasmuch as it was revoked in July, 1858, by the

Commercial Treaty.

This latter treaty was the result of most patient toil on the part of Mr. Harris, and gave a basis for similar treaties, con-

---

¹ A most interesting account of Mr. Harris' reception on this occasion is given in minute details on pp. 621-636, *Foreign Relations*, 1879-80, Vol. I.

cluded in the course of a few years with Great Britain, France, Russia, Holland, and all other nations. The main points in this treaty were as follows: —

TREATY OF AMITY AND COMMERCE.

Signed at Yedo, 29th July, 1858. Ratifications exchanged at Washington, 22nd May, 1860.

I. Peace and friendship. Diplomatic Agent and Consul General. Privileges of residence in Japan; travel beyond treaty limits. Consuls to reside at open ports. Reciprocal privileges to like officials of Japan.

II. Mediation of the United States in differences between Japan and European Powers. Assistance by United States ships of war to Japanese vessels on the high seas, and by United States Consuls in foreign ports.

III. Additional ports to be opened (Kanagawa and Nagasaki, 4th of July, 1859; Niigata, January 1, 1860; Hyogo, January 1, 1863); American citizens may reside therein. Rules and regulations as to their residence. Provisions as to residence of Americans in Yedo and Osaka. Regulations of trade. These provisions to be made public by Japanese Government. Munitions of war; to whom only to be sold: rice and wheat not to be exported from Japan; surplus thereof to be sold to residents, and for ships' crews, &c. Copper surplus to be sold at auction. Americans may employ Japanese.

IV. Duties to be paid according to tariff. Proceedings where there is a difference as to the value of duties. Supplies for United States Navy. Opium prohibited; penalty for smuggling. Imports on which duties are paid may be transported without further tax. No higher duties than are fixed by this treaty.

V. Foreign coins to be current in Japan; may be used in payments; to be exchanged for Japanese coins, etc. Coins, except copper, may be exported; uncoined foreign gold and silver may be exported.

VI. Jurisdiction over offences; Americans against Japanese in Consular Courts; Japanese against Americans by local authorities. Consular Courts open to Japanese creditors. Forfeitures and penalties for violation of treaty. Neither government to be responsible for debts of its subjects or citizens.

VII. Limits of right to travel (10 ri in any direction) from open ports. That American criminals (e. g. convicted of felony) shall lose right of permanent residence in Japan. Such persons to have reasonable time to settle their affairs, to be determined by American Consul.

VIII. Religious freedom. Religious animosity not to be excited.

IX. Japanese authorities, on request of Consul, will arrest deserters and fugitives from justice. Will receive prisoner in jail. Consul to pay just compensation.

X. Japanese Government may purchase or construct vessels of war, etc., in United States. May engage from the United States the services of scientific men and advisers.

XI. Regulations appended (pertaining to trade) make part of treaty.

XII. Conflicting provisions of treaty of March 31, 1854, and the convention of June 17, 1857, repealed. Regulations may be made to carry this treaty into effect.

XIII. Revision of treaty and trade regulations may be made upon one year's notice, at any time after July 1, 1872, if desired by either party.

XIV. Treaty to take effect July 4, 1850. Ratifications to be exchanged at Washington. Signed in English, Dutch and Japanese languages; in case of dispute, Dutch version to be considered the original.

There were appended to this treaty seven separate regulations relating to the custom-house: unloading of goods, revenue frauds, clearance, tonnage duties, fees, import and export duties.

The new commercial treaty must be officially reported to the Emperor, and his sanction obtained. The Shogun's ministers were despatched to receive this, and it was expected that the Emperor would give his approval before September.[1]

The ministers spoke of the necessity of discontinuing the superannuated policy of exclusion, of the perils of the moment, of the disasters in China. Intimations and insinuations, petitions and persuasions, were alike ineffectual. The imperial Nay was backed by a tremendous force of the "Barbarian"-and-Shogun-hating party. Post-haste manifestoes reach the Palace from all quarters, praying the Emperor to undo the convention. He is assured of faithful service, should disagreeable consequences follow. The imperial dignitaries interrogate the Yedo messengers on many a suspicious point. "Does not national sentiment abhor the treaty?" "What do the dates '1854' and '1858,' signed in the treaty, signify? Do they not show that America also is a country of 'evil sect?'" "What security can you give that the Barbarians, whom you allow to reside in Hyogo, will not defame the sacred capital (Kyoto)?" These questions could not be satisfactorily answered, for what will ever satisfy prejudice?

Among the more intelligent of the populace, prejudice was not less strong. Broadsides were posted in the streets, inciting the public to avenge national prestige upon the traitors who befriended "strange folks." Thus, by an unhappy coincidence, the two new platforms—one advocating exclusion and the other foreign intercourse, were identified respectively with the Imperialist and the Shogunate parties. The real issue of this party conflict was—whether Asian tradition or Aryan civilization should triumph. Some there were, who were farsighted enough to support the Imperial restoration and at the same time oppose exclusion, but these were in many instances unfortunate in their end.

Dark as was the cloud that hung over the political horizon

---

[1] It is told by Commodore Tatnall that a sub-treaty was secretly signed by the Premier Ii and Harris, binding them to execute the conditions in the main treaty on Sept. 1, 1858. Griffis, *Perry*, 414.

at this moment, it was not without a silver lining. The
Shogun's embassy[1] to the United States, which was chiefly
planned by Harris, was not without salutary effect.

Growth of Treaty Ports.

According to Article III of the Commercial Treaty, the
port of Kanagawa was opened for foreign trade, but it has
since been surpassed in importance and prosperity by Yokohama. Lieutenant Johnson,[2] writing in 1859 of his previous
visit to Kanagawa, says: "At that time (two or three years
before) nothing could be seen in the way of a town, except a
small cluster of fishermen's huts immediately on the beach;
but as soon as the port was opened for foreign intercourse, it
swarmed with busy mechanics and laborers, building houses,
constructing wharves and bridges, and making every preparation for the accommodation of the thriving commerce which
the sagacious officials foresaw would immediately spring up in
the place."

The present municipality of Yokohama (now numbering
some 115,000 souls, but thirty years ago a mere hamlet), is on
the southern side of the small armlet opening out into Yedo
Bay, distant from Kanagawa two miles by land and three
across the Bay. It then covered about a square mile between
the beach and the marshes on the rear. When the tide rises,
the marshes are turned into a lake, and cut off Yokohama from
the main land. The treaty conceded Kanagawa to foreign
commerce; but, for some reason or other, the native merchants
flocked to the Yokohama side of the Bay. Stores, wharves,
piers, a custom-house, dwellings were all built on that side.[3]
The government apparently favored this tendency, possibly for

---

[1] Detailed account given in the next chapter.
[2] *China and Japan*, 294.
[3] Bishop Smith gives a description of the rapid growth of the port, in his *Ten Weeks in Japan*, p. 280 seq.; also Alcock, *Three Years in Japan*, I, 138-145.

the reason, that, as Kanagawa is on the main road (Tokaido), foreigners, should they reside there, might be liable to more frequent annoyances from anti-foreign factions than at some distance from it. A suspicion naturally arose in the mind of foreign diplomatic agents, that the insular character of Yokohama might be taken advantage of by the Japanese, in restricting the foreign concession and in thus creating a second Deshima! Townsend Harris protested against his countrymen establishing themselves there; but his solicitude was not shared by them. He even threatened to eject those who did not heed his persuasions. The deeper anchorage on the Yokohama side of the Bay, the inducements offered in the form of piers, stores, etc., and the topography of the site, which, unlike Kanagawa, was level, proved more tenable to the calculating reason of traders than the minister's arguments. Harris, finding his efforts futile, requested the Japanese government to refuse Americans the lease of ground in Yokohama. The only advantage gained by this petition was that other foreign residents secured the most eligible building lots! Harris at last abandoned his effort to restrain his countrymen.

Here, then, in Yokohama, was and is transacted most of the foreign trade of Japan. The importance of the place depends, of course, upon its nearness to Tokyo. Two-thirds of its import and export trade pass to and through Tokyo.

Other ports were opened in the course of a few years. Nagasaki, with a population of 40,000, has lost its prestige as *the* port. Kobe-Hyogo grew up like a mushroom, but gives promise of not withering like one. In 1868 Kobe was still a strip of sand, in 1874 its inhabitants numbered 8,500, while at present the two consecutive settlements of Kobe and Hyogo have a population of 104,000. This rapid increase may be accounted for by the superiority of its harbor and its nearness to Kyoto and Osaka. When Kobe was first opened, a merchant of Osaka, together with nineteen coadjutors, was chosen by the government to form a trading corporation, and annual grants of rice were made to them as a subsidy.

Niigata, a town of some 44,000 souls, is almost useless as a treaty port, probably on account of its unfavorable situation and harbor.

Hakodate, 47,000 in population, is important for the exportation of sea products to China.

The relative importance of these ports will be evident from the following table, which gives the percentage of the imports and exports for the five years from 1881 to 1885:

	Yokohama	Kobe-Hyogo	Nagasaki	Hakodate
Exports,	69.	20.	9.3	1.7
Imports,	67.5	28.8	3.4	0.3

The Currency Question (1854–'69).

In our hasty sketch of the Dutch trade, we have seen how abnormal the ratio of gold to silver was in Japan, in the seventeenth and eighteenth centuries. Ever since regular mints (Ginza) were established, in 1601, the ratio has undergone many fluctuations. Still it was always large enough to encourage the exportation of gold. A taste for luxury, novelty and extravagance, "engendered by the Dutch trade"— says an old writer, helped not a little to the efflux of gold, as the balance was always against Japan. Discrepancy in circulation followed. Financial reforms were repeatedly attempted. These invariably consisted not in *reforming* but in *deforming* coinage. Observing the successive depreciations of currency, the shrewder merchants hoarded their specie. The returns of the gold mines of Sado began to diminish. The price of commodities of daily consumption was so small that gold was altogether too valuable to circulate as a medium of exchange, hence it was withdrawn from circulation. Again, the seniorage was charged at an extravagant rate. All these circumstances operated to retire gold from the general market. Still the ratio of gold to silver was 1 : 5-6.

When, in 1854, Perry's squadron anchored in the Yedo Bay, ammunition was needed, but the requisite cash was not to be found in the State vault. Indeed, so empty was the Shogun's treasury, that his old minister has recently expressed the opinion, that, even if left to itself, the Shogunate would, without external cause have perished, within ten years, of bankruptcy. Debasement of coinage, ever the easiest refuge of destitute tyrants, temporarily supplied a large sum. Old silver was melted and coined into *isshiu* (small rectangular coins, face value 6¼ cents). Old gold coins were bought at a premium of seven per cent.; but as this was less than its market value, by more than 18 per cent., there was no inducement for the people to part with them.

Perry stipulated that the Mexican dollar should be exchanged for the *ichibu* (=4 *isshiu*), the silver coin most common in circulation. He did not know that the metallic value of the *ichibu* was only 33 cents in U. S. gold, and that it was only a token money.[1] So, for a time, Americans were losers. Not so, however, after the 5th article of Harris' treaty came into effect, in 1859. According to this article, coins of the same metal were to be exchanged weight for weight. We have seen that the market ratio of gold and silver was then at the abnormal rate of 1:6. Never did Gresham's law operate more briskly. Mexican dollars were exchanged for three *ichibu*, or, more exactly, 100 Mexican dollars were received at the rate of 311 *ichibu*, and these were exchanged for a gold *Koban* at the rate of four *ichibu* to one. The profit aggregated to about 70 per cent., says Mr. Johnson.[2] The *oban* was bought at the rate of $52.50; taken to Hong Kong or Shanghai, it sold for $71.50. The *koban* was purchased at the average of $2.50 and sent to China, where it brought $3.75.

---

[1] Silver coins were greatly overrated in reference to their contents of precious metal, and represented in exchanges a wholly disproportionate value in the two extremes of gold and copper coins. In round numbers, the silver coin was overrated in the proportion of two-thirds, both as regarded the gold and copper currency. Alcock, *Three Years*, II, 348–363; see also I, 147. In Hakodate the ratio of gold to silver was even 4.7:1. Williams' *Life and Letters*, 220.

[2] *China and Japan*, p. 301.

"An American in Japan in 1858,"[1] after boasting of his bargain, "paying only $2.32½ for coin which is intrinsically worth about $9.76," naïvely remarks: " How a Wall Street broker might turn over his Mexican dollars, were he here with his bags, and were there no law against the export of Japanese gold ! "

This traffic in gold was encouraged by the avarice of both parties, the buyer regarding it as an exceedingly satisfactory transaction, if he could receive a gold *koban*, worth about $3.75, for seven, eight or nine *ichibu* ; and the seller deeming it equally satisfactory, if he could obtain so much silver for what was legally worth only four *ichibu*.

While the government changed the Mexican dollars at the rate of 100 to 311 *ichibu* (minus 4 per cent. for coinage) for the foreign legations and consuls, it refused to receive the Mexican dollars from the Japanese at more than 2-2½ *ichibu*. The natural consequence of this was, that the Japanese merchants had to charge higher prices for their wares, in order to cover their loss. Foreign ministers repeatedly remonstrated, but in vain ; the Japanese government continued to regulate the exchange, and the value of $100 oscillated between 220-250 *ichibu*.[2]

The disastrous drain of gold was put an end to, after some five months, by the government's stepping in and putting into practice the suggestion of the American minister. He showed, from the analysis made at the Philadelphia mint, that the silver *ichibu* had a metallic value of 37 U. S. cents, whereas the gold coin of the same denomination contained the value of $1.11, and that the *koban* was worth $4.44. The only remedy he could suggest, was to receive the *koban* and other gold coins at the custom house, at the value accorded by the foreign standard. As to the medium of exchange, it was provided that those foreigners who wanted to have their Mexican dollars

---

[1] *Harper's Monthly*, Vol. 18, p. 289.
[2] Brennwald, *Schweizerische Abordnung nach Japan*, Bern, 1866, p. 29.

changed, should apply at the custom house for an equivalent in silver *ichibu* or for a local paper money, as in Nagasaki. Every day the custom house was crowded with people demanding exchange. The primitive method of minting, however, did not keep up with the demand. Some days, not more than five dollars could be changed. As the names of the parties desiring exchange were required, a long list of men of straw was handed in.[1] The discovery of this trick led to another device. It was declared that only a small proportion of the sum asked for by each individual, could be exchanged. The scheme was soon counteracted by the foreigners. If a certain amount was really needed, they asked for its multiple, calculating the factor of safety.[2] At one time a sum of 1,200,666,-777,888,999,222,321 *ichibu*, was applied for to be exchanged.

Another expediency resorted to in this emergency, was the issue of debased silver *ichibu*, with just enough metal to make it equivalent to the foreign silver of similar denomination. It passed into circulation under the significant appellation of "dolo kin"—*dolo* being a corruption of American *dollar*, and in Japanese meaning *mud* or *slime*. The issue of the "dolo-kin" covered a period extending from 1859 to 1868, and amounted to the sum of 36,275,381 yen. "One (an *ichibu*) before me," says Mr. Fisher,[3] U. S. Consul in 1864, "fresh from the mint, is nearly half green with verdigris and I feel persuaded it contains much whitened copper."

The amount of moneys other than the "dolo-kin" issued from 1860 to 1869, is calculated at more than fifty-nine millions of yen.

The efflux of gold, the debasement of silver coins, the issue of provincial paper money, the unstable condition of the market, the general rise in prices, were some of the immediate effects of the opening of the country to foreign trade. These led to

---

[1] See a humorous description by an eye-witness, Johnston, *China and Japan*, 330.
[2] Cf. Leon Levi, *History of British Commerce*, 384.
[3] *Commercial Relations*, 1864, p. 680.

The Revival of Anti-Foreign Prejudice.

Townsend Harris, writing in 1861, says that since July, 1859, the price of all articles of export from Japan rose from 100 to 300 per cent. The Samurai class (the fighting and consuming corporation) suffered most. As to the daimios, who received their revenue in kind, Harris writes: "When I first came to Yedo in November, 1857, only thirteen of the daimios, out of some three hundred, were in favor of opening the country, while at present about one-half of them are in favor of the new order of things." Henry A. Tilley, an Englishman who visited Nagasaki about 1859, speaks[1] of the prices having doubled there in a very short time, and yet in this town things were cheaper than in others. Silk doubled in value at the ports, during 1860 and '65.[2] The demand for cotton, owing to the American War, raised its price from a few cents to thirty or over thirty cents a pound.[3] Mr. Tilley says that the prices of most articles rose upwards of 500 per cent., in the course of a few months. Of prices in Hakodate, Tronson notes a vast rise after his arrival and before his departure, in 1855.[4]

The political prejudice, which would perhaps better be named the race prejudice, prevalent among the samurai class, was thus envenomed by a sense of economic injustice. When one's pride and purse are attacked, his nerves grow keenly alive, but when the heart of one so injured is poisoned by religious antipathy, what will he not do? To hate a foreigner, became to the samurai an act at once of utility, of loyalty and of piety.

---

[1] Japan, 1856-60, pp. 65, 69.
[2] Scherzer, "Fachmännischen Berichten über die Oesterreichisch-Ungarische Expedition nach Siam, China und Japan," quoted in Liebscher, Japans landwirthsch. u. allgemein wirthschaftl. Verhältnisse, p. 129.
[3] Pumpelly, Across America and Asia, p. 121.
[4] See a tabular account in his Personal Narrative of a Voyage to Japan, p. 360. Eggs rose from $1 to $2 a hundred; fish $1 to $3 a dozen, etc., etc.

I would fain draw a veil over a few years that succeeded the opening of the country. Even so good a friend as Townsend Harris was marked as a victim of conspiracy. In August, 1859, a Russian officer and two sailors were killed in Yokohama. Ten weeks later, a Chinese servant of a French Consul, because he was dressed in European clothes, was slain in that town. Early in the next year, Denkichi, a Japanese linguist in the service of the British Legation, was mortally wounded and soon after died. A month later, two Dutchmen, masters of merchant vessels, were hacked to pieces. On March 23, 1860, the Regent of the Shogun, Ii-Kamon, who had been wielding absolute power for the previous two years, was assassinated on his way to the court. The day of this tragic event is still vividly remembered by many. It has passed into popular literature and supplied many novelists with the plots of their stories. The reason for this assault was explained in the manifesto of the assassins: "That Naosuke Ason (name of the Regent), in arrogance of power, had insulted the Imperial decree, and, careless of the misery of the people, but making foreign intercourse his chief aim, had opened ports, had imprisoned and confined to their houses loyal princes of the blood, nobles of the court and territorial nobles."

Mr. Heusken[1] was the next victim of the merciless foreigner-hunters. While out riding one day in January, 1861, he was fatally wounded. A young man of twenty-nine, he had a widowed mother living in Amsterdam. Townsend Harris suggested to the Japanese government that it should send $10,000 to her, "*not* for the blood of her son, but for her support." This was done.

Heusken was not the last of the sacrifices offered at the altar of "*Jo-i*" (expulsion of foreigners). July 5th and again June 26th, 1862, the British Legation was attacked, and in

---

[1] Mr. Heusken's Diary appears in *German Asiatic Soc. Proceedings*, June, 1883. Eng. trans., *Japan Mail*, Jan. 1884.

the broil which ensued two British marines were killed. In February, 1862, an attempt was made to murder the minister of foreign affairs—Ando, but he escaped with two or three wounds. Hordes of masterless, lawless Samurai, called Ronins, went about exacting money to be used in expelling foreigners.

In view of these anti-foreign demonstrations, it had for some time past been a subject of diplomatic correspondence whether it would not be best to postpone the opening of the city of Yedo to foreigners, for one year from the date fixed in Harris' treaty. It was finally agreed that the opening of Yedo, Hyogo, Osaka and Niigata should be delayed until January 1, 1868.

In the midst of sensational diplomacy, Townsend Harris was released from his duty. Robert H. Pruyn was appointed[1] to succeed Harris, and he arrived in Yedo in April, 1862, in the heat of anti-foreign fanaticism.

The murderous outrages of the Ronins, the Shogun's government was powerless to stop, while they served to confirm to the Imperialists the absurdity of opening the country. In June, 1862, special envoys were dispatched from Kyoto to announce the will of the Emperor to expel the "Barbarians." The next year, the Shogun was summoned to Kyoto to give account of his stewardship. During his absence from Yedo, the tables were turned; new appointments were made in his cabinet, the compulsory residence of daimios in Yedo was relaxed, "in consequence of which," says a native writer, "all the resident daimios and other officials sent their wives and children to their country estates, and, in the twinkling of an eye, the flourishing city of Yedo became like a desert."

---

[1] It is almost pathetic to read Secretary Seward's letter to Mr. Pruyn at his appointment, for it was immediately after the outbreak of the Civil War, and Mr. Seward's instructions read like a father's parting words to his son, as he leaves the threshold of an unquiet family to launch on a dangerous voyage. See *Diplomatic Correspondence*, 1862, p. 817.

In Kyoto, to the *daimios* assembled, an Imperial decree was read, the purport of which was the speedy expulsion of foreigners. The 25th of June, 1863, was fixed as the day for final expulsion. An answer in the affirmative was extorted from the Shogun. When the day arrived (the Shogun was still detained in Kyoto), an abrupt communication was made by his minister in Yedo, to the foreign representatives. It reads:

"I communicate with you by a dispatch. The orders of the Tycoon received from Kyoto, are to the effect that the ports are to be closed and the foreigners driven out, because the people of the country do not desire intercourse with foreign countries. The discussion of this has been entirely entrusted to me by His Majesty. I therefore send this communication first, before holding the conference respecting the details."

Signed.

Such a dispatch was tantamount to a declaration of war. Fortunately, however, the foreign representatives were well aware that this communication did not convey the sincere sentiment of the Shogunate. A few weeks previously, the British and French envoys, knowing the attitude of the Shogun, offered assistance to him against the Imperial Party. The American envoy was not consulted on the subject. Prudently the Shogunate ministry declined the offer. Only three weeks before the above dispatch was sent, alluding to an attack on the British Legation, a Japanese minister had said, not without an appearance of sincerity: "We hope that affairs likely to break off the intercourse between the two countries, may not again arise." From this fact, the foreign envoys gathered that the dispatch was intended only as mock obedience to the Imperial mandate.

Meanwhile the Shogun returned to Yedo. He reported to Kyoto his utter inability to comply with the sacred order of expelling foreigners, and begged to resign his position. This was in August. The next month, the Netherlands and the

United States ministers were invited to a secret conference with the Council of Elders. Favors were asked through them of all foreign representatives, to confine trade to Nagasaki and Hakodate, and to close Yokohama. Such proposals could not of course be listened to.

All this while the foreign envoys, with the exception of Mr. Pruyn, resided in Yokohama. He did not leave Yedo until sheer necessity compelled him to do so. On the 24th of May, 1863, the American Legation was set on fire, and Mr. Pruyn barely escaped with the official archives. He still persisted in residing in Yedo and found temporary shelter in a temple, but, being warned within a week of an immediate assault of ronin, he sought safety on board a Japanese steamer and was taken to Yokohama. The U. S. Consul and missionaries were also advised instantly to leave Yedo for their own security. The patience of the American Minister may well have been exhausted by these wrongs, aggravated by others of a more private character. In May, 1863, one Mr. Shoyer— a resident American merchant—was threatened by his Japanese employés. Mr. Stearns was attacked by a mob and severely bruised. A Mr. Robertson was seized in his sick-bed, by natives, and forcibly carried off to a swamp. As satisfaction for these injuries and insults, Mr. Pruyn demanded a payment of $20,000. In addition, a sum of $10,000 was asked for the personal loss he sustained when the Legation was burnt. Another $1,000 was also demanded as indemnity for the rough treatment inflicted on one Horton, in Bonin Island, and $1,200 for the Pembroke claim. The settlement of these claims was, after some reluctance, secured.

True, in enforcing these claims, Mr. Pruyn had often to remind the Council of Elders that any breach of the treaty would eventuate in war, unless it were satisfied by a sacrifice of money or right. But he had no display of American navy in Japanese waters.[1] Through the most trying moments of

---

[1] Of course, absence of U. S. men-of-war in Japanese waters at that time must not be attributed merely to American good will. They were needed at home, and abroad there was some fear of an *Alabama* experience.

diplomacy, he never deviated from his principle, namely, "the utmost moderation," which, in his own words, "was the best policy." So closely did he cling to this principle, that he was once suspected by his British colleague of complicity with the Japanese.

Decline of Anti-Foreign Ideas.

The year 1862 has already been mentioned, as a year when murder stalked abroad in quest of its victims. Foreigners were cautioned from giving any cause of irritation to the infuriated *Jo-i* men. Notwithstanding this, a party of three Englishmen and a lady, riding out one day in September, and happening to meet a train of the *daimio* (Satsuma), behaved in a most imprudent manner. Seeing the approach of the procession, the party spoke of turning back, but was dissuaded by one of its number, a young merchant from Shanghai. Confident that he knew "how to treat *these people*," he led the party in front of the procession, when the escort of. of the *daimio* took their behavior as an insult, ran after them, and "treated" with a slash of a keen blade the fated braggart. The others escaped, the two men being slightly wounded, while the lady was not touched. The consequence of the "treatment" was the "Richardson Affair," so named from the victim. It implied the payment of $500,000 from the Shogunate and $125,000 from Satsuma, and the surrender of the murderers. Non-compliance with these demands gave rise to the bombardment of Kagoshima, the seat of the Satsuma daimiate, in August, 1863, by an English squadron. A hard lesson did the campaign prove to be to the *daimio* of Satsuma. Not only was the required indemnity paid in solid cash, but the batteries, factories and dwellings were leveled to the ground, and many a Japanese life, no less precious than the young merchant's, was sacrificed. In the school of experience, the most useful lesson is generally the hardest. Considering what followed this experience, the most parsimonious will not deem a tuition of $625,000 too dear. Satsuma had up to this time been a ringleader of the anti-foreign party. When their capital was bombarded, her brave sons did their best, but when they found, to their mortification, that the "barbarians" were more than a match for them and beheld, to their shame, their strongholds reduced to ashes, then—but not till then, were they convinced of the superiority of Westerners. Once convinced, the *samurai* of Satsuma, with their characteristic energy, became the advocates of occidental civilization.

Another page of bitter lesson was still reserved for the *dcrimio* of Nagato (Choshiu). A stern foe of foreigners and of the Shogun, he harbored the political malcontents of the Empire. In June, 1863, an American merchant steamer, on its way to Shanghai, was passing over forbidden waters near Shimonoseki in the province of Nagato, when it was suddenly fired upon. Ten days later the same thing happened to a French man-of-war. Soon after, a Dutch corvette received the same treatment. "At the instigation of the over-zealous English envoy (Sir Rutherford Alcock)," says Professor Rein,[1] "although England had not been injured by Choshiu and the honor of the other three nations had received full satisfaction, a great fleet was assembled, consisting of nine English, three French, four Dutch and one American man-of-war, and Shimonoseki was bombarded on the 5th and 6th of September, 1864." The result was the demand of an indemnity of three million dollars—$785,000 each to France, Holland and the United States and the rest to Great Britain,—to be paid according to the convention signed October 22, 1864, in quarterly instalments of one-sixth. These powers were, however, afterward induced to decrease the sum by one-half. The Shimonoseki affair, as the whole concern is called, converted Nagato from the error of its ways and made it a staunch friend of Western progress.

---

[1] *Japan*, Vol. I. Eng. Trans., p. 350.

About this time, too (August, 1864), returned from Europe the embassy which had been sent by the Shogunate to request the European governments that Japan might close the ports. They brought home the astounding news of the discovery they had made, namely: that "it was not the foreigners, but we ourselves that are barbarians." Traitorous sounded these words, and the newsbearers were divested of their trust.

A report of a similar discovery was made by the daimio of Echizen, in 1865. In his memorial to the Emperor, he says: "Western foreigners of to-day differ essentially from those of former times. They are much more cultivated and liberal. . . . . There are five powerful continents, and even if all Japan were united, it would be shattered like a roofing tile."

It was evident, too, that the foreign traders manifested no special inclination to carry rice out of the country. It had been a matter of gravest solicitude, lest, if foreign trade were opened, the native markets would be drained of this "staff of life," and that its price would rise exorbitantly. The treaty of 1858 contained a special provision that rice and wheat should not be exported.[1]

Among other causes contributing to weaken the anti-foreign prejudices, may be enumerated the impressions which the native officials received in their personal intercourse with foreigners, and the differences between the doctrines and precepts preached by the Protestant missionaries and those taught by the Catholics.

Nor must the influence of Holland be left out of consideration in this matter. Mention has been made of the letters from King William II to the Shogun, in 1844, and again in 1852. Even years before these dates Siebold had written— "Being the only state which has friendly relations with Japan, Holland must take upon itself the responsibility of opening Japan to the commerce of all other commercial nations."[2]

---

[1] The exportation of rice and wheat, and the flours of the same, was allowed after the beginning of August, 1873, free of customs (export) duty.

[2] Nippon, *Archiv zur Beschreibung von Japan*, Abtheil VI, p. 43.

Thus by strange and steep ways was the party of Imperialists brought to a common ground with the Shogunate—respect and good will towards foreigners. The issue of the party contest now turned on the restoration of the Emperor or the preservation of the Shogunate.

The real attitude of the Shogun towards the Emperor gradually became more and more clear to foreigners. It was, however, most plainly demonstrated by a German resident, who, in his "Open Letter to the Representatives of Western Nations at Yedo," says that "the reason why the Tycoon breaks his promise is because *he cannot keep it*, and the reason why he cannot keep it is because *he had no right to give it*."[1] Mr. Pruyn had several times felt that it was of vital importance to obtain the sanction of the Mikado to the treaties. He frequently urged the Shogun to exert his influence to this end. Mr. Pruyn was not alone in this idea and at last, in November, 1865, with all the pomp and dignity becoming so momentous an occasion, the English, French, Dutch and American envoys proceeded to Hyogo by sea. They at once commenced negotiations with the court in Kyoto for the immediate ratification of the treaties by the Emperor himself. Equivocation could not avail. If the voice of the Powers were too low to be heard, cannons could speak as loud as Japan would care to hear. The Imperial "Nay" was no longer backed by an anti-foreign party. "Yes" was the only answer that wise policy and national safety could utter. In the same month, the Envoys succeeded in obtaining the formal sanction of the treaties from the Emperor.

This act of the Imperial ratification was a death blow to anti-foreignism. As the hostile attitude of the Emperor had been the mainstay of the *Jo-i* party, so the change in his position produced corresponding results in the minds of many of his subjects.

---

[1] For further extracts from this letter, see Mossman, *New Japan*, pp. 142, 143.

The following year (1866) treaties with Italy and Belgium were signed.[1] The same year (May 23d) restrictions upon travel abroad were repealed; passports were issued for any who might desire to go abroad. This right of foreign travel was, together with the liberty of Japanese merchants to trade in foreign countries without interference of officers, emphatically declared in the Tariff Convention of June, 1866. It was announced that Japanese Legations would be established in foreign capitals.

But, within the country, peaceful reforms were not the only features of the years immediately following the Imperial ratification. Far from it! The Revolution—the last struggle of the Shogunate for self-preservation—marked the era which was happily consummated in

The Restoration of the Imperial Authority,

in January, 1868. Some of the Treaty Powers at first looked with suspicion upon the ascendency of the Imperial (the whilom anti-foreign) party. During the Revolutionary War, the foreign nations proclaimed their neutrality, but their secret sympathies were with the Shogunate. Indeed, a few French naval tacticians were in the actual employ of the rebel party. Secretary Seward confessed years after, that "I used all the influence I had to prevent the late revolution in Japan, because I thought it was a retrograde movement; I little dreamed that the restored Mikado would excel the dethroned Tycoon in emulating the Western civilization."[2]

---

[1] Those with Prussia and Holland were signed in 1860.

[2] His *Travels*, p. 257. But let it be noticed that the action of the American representative, as well as the advice of Mr. Seward as Secretary of State, was most impartial. Before the Civil War broke out, the Shogun had purchased of the United States an iron-clad ram, the *Stonewall*, at $400,000. When it reached Yokohama in April, 1868, under the Japanese colors, it was claimed by the two belligerent parties. In view of the strict neutrality, it remained under the American flag until peace was reëstablished.

Once converted to the belief of the superiority of Western civilization, the Imperial government pursued with unrelenting energy the policy of its introduction. The first interview between the Emperor and the foreign envoys was held on the 23d of January, 1868, when "they congratulated His Majesty on the magnificence of the Imperial rule, and gave renewed promise of friendly relations." The summer of the same year saw the Imperial seat removed to Yedo, which name was henceforth changed to Tokyo (Eastern Capital—in contrast to Kyoto, which was afterwards called Saikyo or Western Capital). From this date begins the present year-period, *Mei-ji* (Enlightened Reign). Three years after, the Daimios gave up their fiefs of their own free will; feudalism was thus abolished. The army and navy were necessarily reorganised, and a new code was promulgated; coinage took a new form; embassies were sent to Treaty Powers; postal and telegraph systems were introduced and common school regulations were enforced; lighthouses and railroads were built; the interdiction of Christianity disappeared; the new era of liberty was ushered in and the germ of constitutional government was sown.[1] It would be an endless task to enumerate the changes which Japan has seen since the revolution of 1868. In the words of an American journalist, "It is too little to say that, during the last half dozen years, Japan has made more history for itself than in the preceding two and a half centuries of its own annals. It has exhibited transformations, the like of which have required ages to accomplish in any other land."[2] Those years of reconstruction were far from being free from "blind impetuosity," "costly innovations," "irrational attempts" and "useless experiments;" but what nation can boast of immunity from errors of one kind or another, when it is called upon to heal the wounds of a civil war and simul-

---

[1] Cf. Mr. Wigmore's interesting sketch of representative institutions in Japan, in the *Nation*, July 24, 1890.
[2] Howe, in *Harper's Magazine*, Vol. 46, p. 856.

taneously to maintain its position against threatening foreign powers clamoring at its doors?

The Shimonoseki Indemnity.

The incident which led to the payment by the Japanese Government of three million dollars, as indemnity to England, France, Holland and the United States of America, has already been noted. A clause in the convention touching the affair, dated October 22, 1864, stated very generously that it was no object of the Powers to mulct Japan in pecuniary indemnities, but to establish *better relations*, and to place these on a more satisfactory and mutually advantageous footing. They would be so gracious, they said, as to be content with the opening of Shimonoseki or some other port in the Inland sea. The proud spirit of Japan forbade her from surrendering a right, but money, trash abstractly (though a round sum of three millions was too concrete a reality), she would pay. The first instalment was paid in August, 1865, and the second and third in January and May of the following year. By this time, owing to various causes—some of which have been touched upon in the course of the present paper, the Shogun's government found that its pride cost it rather too dear, and asked that the payment of the balance might be deferred until 1872. In consequence of the ready manner in which the Council of Elders accepted the new convention and tariff which were then proposed, the four Powers gave up altogether the claim on the remainder.

The share allotted to the United States in the three million indemnity, was $785,000. This was several times more than the damages done her, which only amounted to $19,929. Soon after the event, before the four Powers coalesced, the United States Minister had demanded $32,000. We have seen that by far the chief part of the operation was played by the British. That the distribution of the indemnity was equally made, was due to Earl Russell's policy—that, inasmuch as all powers concerned had interest in common, they should share alike. This apparently generous action of the British Government was the beginning of the diplomatic coalition,—a principle to which the foreign representatives hang closely in their dealings with the East.

Of the whole amount paid by Japan, one-fourth ($586,125.06) was received by the United States. This was invested at par in the ten-forty bonds of the United States Government, in which was also invested the accruing interest, and, in 1872, the fund amounted to $706,000 in registered bonds.

When Mr. Mori, *Chargé d'Affaires* at Washington, was informed that this sum lay in a coffer in the Department of State and that it might be returned to Japan, he assured his American friends that, should it be repaid, it would be put to educational uses at home. Thereupon Mr. Lanman suggested that the best way to get the question before Congress for scientific action, would be through Professor Joseph Henry of the Smithsonian Institution. Professor Henry was only too glad to exert his influence in so honorable a cause. His memorial (1870) to the Library Committee of Congress for the return of the above sum to Japan, to be devoted to educational purposes, circulated widely among College presidents[1] and others interested in the subject, and called forth hearty approval, the only discussion being as to the conditions to be attached to the return. President Julius H. Seelye would have had it spent for the advancement of female education in Japan; Mr. Daniel C. Gilman, then president of the State University of California, naturally enough preferred to invest the sum in some American institution on the Pacific coast, where oriental students could have easy access.[2] Hon. B. G. Northrop, LL. D., advocated its return without any condition.

---

[1] *House Misc.*, 42d Cong., 3d session, Vol. II.; also *Sen. and House Misc. Doc.*, 44th Cong., 2d session.
[2] *Overland Monthly*, Vol. X, p. 184.

Not only professional educators but also the mercantile community, notably the New York Chamber of Commerce,[1] raised its voice in support of repayment. Secretary Wm. H. Seward and Minister DeLong warmly approved it. The press had some generous words to say. Mr. Lanman, in his capacity as Secretary of the Japanese Legation, together with a special attorney engaged for the purpose, brought all the influence he could to bear upon the return. Dr. Northrop wrote, lectured and preached for ten years to secure the repayment, and he went before each successive Committee on Foreign Affairs on the subject. The Committee of the House reported as follows: "It is believed that such a policy (remittance) will result in the re-establishment of more intimate relations between this government and the government of Japan, and ultimately prove of great benefit to the commerce of the two countries and accelerate the progress of civilization."[2]

By the unanimous consent of the whole nation, in fulfilment of the Act of Congress, February 22, 1883, was the sum of $785,000 reimbursed to Japan, giving another evidence of the liberal and sympathizing policy of America towards Japan. It is slanderous to suspect that this was done from any interested motive on the part of the United States. There is no doubt that she could well afford it; but, so far as ability to afford is concerned, the other powers involved in the Shimonoseki affair are far from being unable. This action of the United States government will be a standing protest against the accusation that "Americanism" is nothing more than commercialism.

Tariff Convention.

The Shimonoseki Indemnity was not the only immediate issue of the rash and untimely act of the Nagato samurai.

---

[1] *Senate Misc.*, 44th Cong., 1st session, Vol. I.
[2] Report of the Committee of the House of Representatives, 1871-72, Vol. 3, No. 79.

The sharp diplomats were on the alert to reap every advantage from any mishap. Seeing how the poor Shogunal government was burdened with so many ills from within and without, until it bent its head under their weight, the representatives of four Christian nations sought to make the weight still heavier. With the extortion of a Shylock and the wisdom of a Portia, they worked until they succeeded in turning the emergency of Japan to their petty commercial interests. Better to understand this story of the Tariff Convention, we must cast a glance at the Regulations regarding trade and commerce, which were attached to the commercial treaty of 1858.

In these Regulations, the registry of ships, trans-shipping of cargo, custom-house formalities, etc., may well be passed over in silence here. What interests us, is Regulation VII, which gives the schedule of articles on which duties are levied. Class I, includes articles free of duty; silver and gold, wearing apparel in actual use, household furniture and printed books for private use. Class II, pays five per cent. duty, and has reference to articles used in building, rigging or fitting out of ships, salted provisions, breadstuffs, living animals, coals, building timber, rice, paddy, steam machinery, zinc, lead, tin and raw silk. Class III, meaning intoxicating liquors, pays a duty of thirty-five per cent. Articles not mentioned in the above three classes pay twenty per cent. Articles of Japanese production, exported as cargo, pay five per cent., with the exception of gold and silver coins and copper in bars. The whole Regulation closes with the sentence: "Five years after the opening of Kanagawa, the import and export duties shall be subject to revision, if the Japanese government desires it."

Certainly the last clause was apparently very kindly put, and the four Powers who had succeeded in threatening and wresting the Shimonoseki indemnity, were bent upon taking advantage of this generous provision. In November, 1865, they said, the Japanese government gave a written engagement to the representatives of these Powers in Osaka, to revise the tariff on the general basis of a duty of five per cent. on the value of all articles imported or exported, for the Japanese government was "desirous of affording a fresh proof of its wish to promote trade and to cement the friendly relations which exist between their country and foreign nations." Certainly a queer way to manifest friendly feeling,—too self-denying to be statesmanlike! The representatives of France, Great Britain, the Netherlands and the United States, proceeded to fulfil this wish of the Japanese government, and the result was the Tariff Convention, signed on the 25th of June, 1866. This came into effect in five days, and was subject to revision on the 1st of July, 1872. According to this convention, all articles of imports were divided into four classes,—the first including those that pay very low specific duties, comprising almost entirely manufactured articles; the second, free goods; the third, prohibited goods (opium, to wit); the fourth, goods subject to an *ad valorem* duty of five per cent. on original value. A table of tariff on exports is similarly classified.

Trade and Commerce.

At the time when Perry's expedition was only maturing in idea, one W. D. Porter predicted that a direct trade with Japan would increase the commerce of the United States about $200,000,000 annually, if not more. Mr. Spalding, writing soon after his return from the expedition, did not scruple to call this prophecy "a mere myth existing in the brain of visionaries alone."[1] What Mr. Spalding said turned out to be right.

At first the foreign trade of Japan was so jealously watched by the officials, that, when an evasive or smuggling merchant was detected, he was even deemed worthy of capital punishment. Then, too, the practice of two centuries and a half had so trained the people, that, when the commercial treaty

---

[1] *Japan Expedition*, p. 357.

was completed, they looked upon any dealing with foreigners as out of the pale of their rights, and only by special explanations from the state could they—that is to say a large number of them—be persuaded to take an active part in the new enterprise. The Shogunate regarded foreign trade as a matter of state concern—a government monopoly. The treaty was a contract between the two governments, the *people* had no voice in it; the third estate was nothing. J. M. Tronson gives an account of what he saw at this time. He says[1] that all the merchandise was brought to a bazaar, which was opened every morning with a tedious official ceremony and closed in the evening in the same manner. All transactions were supervised by an official, and every particular was noted in an official ledger. Such a cumbrous way of traffic, could not, however, continue long. The market was soon nominally open to the public, although it was still constantly watched.

Among the grievances of the trading community we find enumerated[2] the defect in the construction of cargo-boats, the inadequate number of boatmen and coolies, the transaction of business only by licensed merchants, limited supply of silk and tea, restrictions in the sale of cocoons, official interference in the purchase and delivery of goods and depreciation of Mexican dollars, due to the action of the government in forcing the people to exchange them at a low rate. These inconveniences and restrictions were shortly removed or remedied; but others took their place. Placards were sometimes hung in the streets of Kyoto and Osaka, forbidding the sale of silk, tea or cotton, to foreigners. This was probably a ruse of persons who had bought up all the silk, that they might unsettle the price and then bring out their goods.

Whether from the removal of official restrictions alone or from other causes as well, the trade in 1863 doubled, as com-

---

[1] See, for fuller description, Tronson's *Personal Narrative of a Voyage to Japan*, pp. 357, 358. Cf. Spalding, *Japan Expedition*, p. 334.
[2] Adams, *History of Japan*, Vol. I, p. 168.

pared with the previous year. But, until the Centennial Exhibition, American-Japanese commerce did not assume any importance, and even since then it has been far from satisfactory.

The increase of trade between the two countries is shown in the following table:

	From Japan to U. S. A. in 1000 Yen.	From U. S. A. to Japan in 1000 Yen.	Proportion of	
			U.S. Imports to Japan in Percentage of Total.	Japanese Exports to U.S.
1885	15,639	3,246	10	42
1886	19,988	4,258	11	41
1887	22,243	4,134	8	42
1888	23,475	5,673	9	36
1889	26,109	6,173	9	37

To give some idea of the total foreign trade of Japan we give here its value in millions of yen:

	1884.	1885.	1886.	1887.	1888.
Imports,	29.6	29.3	32.1	44.2	65.4
Exports,	34.0	37.1	48.0	51.5	64.9

Of all the countries trading with us, the United States is our largest customer, buying yearly some 23 millions worth, whereas the next largest buyer, China, receives less than half this amount, and England, which is our greatest seller (imports from England in 1887 and 1888 were 23.7 and 28.7 millions respectively), imports but little from Japan.

Various causes were and are at work to bring about this unfavorable "balance of trade" for America.[1] To densely populated European countries, foreign trade is their life-blood, while to the Americans, protected in their manufactures, and with their daily increasing population, home demand is quite

---

[1] Cf. *Consular Reports*, July, 1886, No. 65.

sufficient for their enterprise; hence, while the European manufacturers cater to Japanese taste, the Americans do not. The mail subsidies to steamship lines enable European merchants to have their goods freighted more cheaply. Political favoritism, too, is a strong influence in deciding which nation shall be the best seller.[1] Again, just as the foreign commerce of Japan began, the civil war in America broke out, and war always cripples commerce as well as everything else. Many articles of American make are too expensive for Japanese demand. The manufacturing districts of the States being on the Atlantic, the surplus of their products find their way across that ocean. The use of intermediate agencies in business transactions between the Americans and the Japanese, is another hindrance to trade.

Japanese Exports to America.

SILK.[2]—Prior to the opening of the Empire to foreign trade in 1859, the annual production of silk was estimated at about 40,000 piculs.[3] The quality was excellent and the price low. The supply was just enough for home consumption. As soon as the country was opened, the price rose nearly 100 per cent. and the quality deteriorated; the production increased about 8 per cent. per annum, the estimate for the season 1861-2 being 50,500 piculs. The aristocracy could not look with favor upon the rise in the price of silk, they being the chief consumers of the commodity. A more serious disturbance of the trade, was the hostile attitude assumed by the ronin toward the native merchants dealing with foreigners.[4] Some silk merchants were driven from their houses, others were even killed. The paternal government issued, in 1860, a circular declaring that all merchandise must first be brought to Yedo, "to be there examined and approved for sale," before it can

---

[1] See *London Economist*, June 25, 1887.
[2] Cf. *Commercial Relations*, 1862, p. 608.
[3] 1 picul = 133⅓ lbs. av.
[4] Cf. *Diplomatic Correspondence*, 1864, p. 449.

enter Yokohama. Three years later, alarmed at the scarcity of silk, it warned all merchants to "regard the future of Japan" and "act accordingly, for the benefit of the country at large." Silk was one of the two articles, the other being tea, which most attracted the attention of American merchants in Japan. But, until the Centennial Exhibition, it was an insignificant item of import. Of the whole quantity of raw silk [1] imported into the United States, amounting to 10,000 bales annually, previous to the Centennial, only one-tenth came from Japan and Europe. For eight years previous to 1876, the annual average of the import of the Japan silk into the States was 97 bales, and in that year only 88 bales were sold in New York. The Exhibition served as an advertisement. The Doshin Silk Company seized the opportunity, and ever since the business has been of steady and healthy growth, until to-day Japan raw silk forms 50 per cent. of all the silk consumed in the United States. From 88 bales in 1876, the import of Japan silk grew to 15,000 (value $9\frac{1}{2}$ million dollars) in 1885. The excellent quality of the cocoon, the cheap skilled labor, the inexhaustible supply of water in silk-producing districts, the adoption of many recent improvements in reeling, promise a further extension of the industry at home.

TEA.—For some time after foreign trade was opened, Japanese tea intended for America was first sent to China to be refined and packed.[2] Afterward the necessary materials were imported and the work was done in Yokohama. The beginning of the tea trade was exceedingly humble, amounting to only 288,000 pounds in the season of 1861–2. Since then, it has shown no sign of retrogression. It is displacing the Chinese green tea in American markets. Of some 85,000,000 pounds annually consumed in the States, more than 40,000,000 pounds are supplied from Japan, and as the cost of transportation decreases this proportion increases. Before

---

[1] See *Am. Journal of Fabrics and Dry Goods Bulletin*, Oct. 30, 1886.
[2] *Diplomatic Correspondence*, 1863, p. 959.

1886, most of the tea sent to the States came by way of the Suez Canal, taking sixty days. A small proportion was carried over the Pacific, costing three cents per pound in a steamer, and 1.75 cents in a sailing vessel. In that year, the competition between the two routes reduced the cost per steamer to 1.75 cents and to 1.25 per sailing vessel, whereupon the number of tea-ships through the Suez was reduced to two. At present[1] there are four lines of competition, reducing the cost of transportation to 1.25 cents per pound from Japan to New York. One draw-back to the increasing favor for Japan tea is the disreputable practice among some dealers of adulterating it.[2] For this, however, the Japanese alone must not bear the blame.[3]

OTHER ITEMS OF EXPORT.—Fans ($110,000 annually), bric-à-brac, lacquer-ware ($50,000), and bronze ($40,000), are some of the rest of the commodities imported into the States. Our straw braid is said to be fast taking the place of the celebrated Mackinaw braids in American markets.[4] In fact, in 1887, $316,000 worth was imported from Japan, though the amount has since decreased. Sulphur, now imported from Italy into the United States, may reasonably be supplied by Japan. In 1889 some $300,000 worth was sent from our country—the largest quantity ever exported by us to America. Camphor is another item of importance, and, in 1889, the United States purchased it to the amount of $340,000. Porcelain ware is sent to America—its sale amounting annually to some $300,000—in 1889, to $398,000.

---

[1] An extract from the N. Y. Tribune in the Public Opinion of October 9, 1886, gives a brief sketch of the tea carriage.

[2] Of the efforts made in Japan to prevent such dishonesty, see in The Bradstreet's, April 19, 1884, extract from the Japan Mail.

[3] Mr. Fisher, United States Consul in Nagasaki, testifies that no coloring matter is used by the natives (Commercial Relations, 1875-6, p. 1105). Mr. Newwitter, Consul in Hyogo, writes of "a foreign firm at this port employing a large number of Chinamen for the purpose of coloring." (Com. Rel., 1877, p. 710).

[4] Cf. Consular Reports, Jan., 1886.

American Imports into Japan.

The only material of special notice is Petroleum. It was first introduced into Yokohama, in 1868, when there were entered at the custom house 2,700 cases, valued at some $6,000. Its spread has been astonishingly rapid. From being an article of luxury twenty years ago, it is now deemed a necessity.[1] A few wells in Echigo, Omi and Hokkaido are utterly inadequate to supply the demand. The importations steadily increased from 4,000 cases in 1870 to 980,000 in 1880. In 1883, the government prohibited the sale of kerosene for illuminating purposes, under burning test of 115° Fahrenheit. In the summer of 1888, the Baku oil was imported for the first time, as a sample, and since then it is more or less gaining ground; still, American petroleum continues to be the chief supply. Out of some 6,143,000 dollars worth of imports, 3,783,000 dollars represented petroleum.

Among other American articles of import, are clocks and watches, the value of which amounted, in 1888, to $415,000, and, in 1889, to $371,000.

The next article of importance is leather and shoes. Nearly $300,000 worth is annually sent from the States to Japan. The import of flours from America has recently been steadily increasing, amounting, in 1889, to some $182,000. Cigarettes likewise form quite an article of commerce. In 1887, the quantity sent was only $18,000, in 1888, $28,000, and, in 1889, $64,000.

Among other articles worthy of mention are the dairy products, books, quicksilver, pencils, lamps, canning and paper machines.

Friendly Diplomacy.

It is often sneeringly stated, and this not without ground, that the United States has no diplomacy. She is no doubt the more blessed on that very account.

---

[1] Cf. *Consular Reports*, Jan., 1884, No. 37.

A New York writer[1] has in indirect terms reprimanded the inconsistency of the Federal Government, when it refused to arbitrate between Russia and Japan on the question of Saghalien, which, according to one of the articles of the treaty, it ought to have done. Mr. Seward also equivocated when he was asked to perform a similar favor.[2] This "sin of omission," on the part of a country bred in the doctrine of Washington and Monroe, may well be excused, the more heartily when we remember that it is this very doctrine which keeps her from a "sin of commission."

The most wholesome influence that can be exerted upon a young individual or nation, is to awaken in him, or it, self-respect and a manly sense of independence. Such it has always been the policy of United States diplomacy to do in Japan. Whatever else changed at each change of the Administration, this never changed. Hence in the rather patronizing statement of General Grant, there is much truth. Speaking[3] of the service of Judge John A. Bingham, for thirteen years (1872–85) the United States minister in Tokyo, he says: "He (Mr. Bingham) has taught the people of Japan that they are a nation, and has taught the nations of the earth to respect them as such." All honor to the veteran Judge from Ohio!

Let us briefly see what he did. He was the first to break loose from the diplomatic coöperation, which was a sort of machinery whereby Christian nations coalesced, when they made blustering demands upon Japan.

When, in February, 1874, the Japanese government issued customs regulations without consulting foreign consuls, Mr. Bingham alone defended Japan's right to do so.

---

[1] Mr. House, Martyrdom of an Empire, *Atlantic Monthly*, 1881.
[2] His *Travels* edited by Olive R. Seward, p. 58.
[3] "*The Current*," Dec. 5, 1885. Mr. Grant says: "I have never made an appointment of which I feel so proud as that of Minister Bingham to Japan."

In October, 1878, when a request was made by the Governor of Kanagawa that all merchant vessels arriving at that port via Nagasaki, where cholera was raging, should be inspected by a medical officer and, if need be, quarantined, and when the consuls of different nationalities objected to the exercise of any other authority by the Japanese government than the mere inspection, the Hon. Bingham declared that such an action "did not accord with the policy of the United States in Japan, nor with our obligations to respect and observe the laws of Japan, and that the action of the consuls is a substantial denial of the undoubted right of this (Japanese) government to prevent the importation of pestilence by foreign vessels into the territorial vessels of Japan."

In the summer of the next year, a German vessel—the Hesperia, was, in defiance of the regulations, taken out of the quarantine by the German consul, who was attended by a man-of-war. General Grant remarked on this occasion, that the vessel ought to have been sunk. Mr. Bingham resented the audacity of the consul on the ground that, should the epidemic be imported, the lives of those under his protection (i. e. the American residents) would be imperilled. But, since his authority extended only over his fellow countrymen, Minister Bingham alone of the foreign representatives recognized in a weaker nation the right which is the only solace of the poorest man—namely, the right to do right.

When the regulations for the sale of opium were issued in October, 1878, they called forth considerable comment from the foreign press in Yokohama, most of which was of an unfavorable nature. The British and French ministers regarded some of the regulations as derogatory to the almighty extraterritorial rights! Not so thought the American representative. Examples of the kind may be increased.

When Japan proposed to sign postal and telegraphic conventions, the United States government was the only treaty power which did not hesitate to recognize her claim and her ability.

The return of the Shimonoseki Indemnity was another link which joined the United States and Japan in a closer bond of friendship.

Indeed, the friendly feeling of the two nations was not restricted to their direct intercourse. During the disturbance at Seoul, Corea, in December, 1884, several Japanese subjects barely escaped the violence of the mob by taking refuge in the U. S. Legation, and such as were taken prisoners were released at the instance of General Lucius H. Foote, U. S. Minister to Corea. In return, during the conflagration on the night of the 23d February, 1885, in the same capital, a Japanese commander promptly detailed his troops to the protection of the American Legation.

It has been remarked by a close student of American institutions, that, "despite the admiration for military exploits which the Americans have sometimes shown, no country is at bottom more pervaded by a hatred of war, and a sense that national honor stands rooted in national fair dealing."[1] American policy in the Far East is an emphatic illustration of this remark—a policy of the nation, and not of any political party or administration. "It was our policy,"—so writes John Russel Young, ex-Minister to China—"it was our policy, I may say the law of the commercial existence of our Pacific Empire, that the autonomy of China and Japan should be maintained; that the sphere of English influence in Asia should cease at Singapore."[2]

The same sentiment was repeatedly expressed by General Grant. In speaking of American policy in Japan, he once said: "Whatever her influence may be, I am proud to think that it has always been exerted in behalf of justice and kindness."[3] Neither is there a lack of response to this cordial feeling of the American nation. In one of the interviews

---

[1] Bryce, *American Commonwealth*, Vol. II, 472.
[2] *North American Rev.*, Aug., 1890, p. 197.
[3] Young, *Around the World with Gen. Grant*, II, 441.

between H. M. the Emperor of Japan and General Grant, the former is reported to have said, "America and Japan being near neighbors, separated by an ocean only, will become more and more closely connected with each other as time goes on."[1]

In this age of steam, an ocean is a means whereby lands are united instead of being separated, and well is the body of water that lies between Japan and America called the Ocean of Great Peace.

But the pacific and friendly relations of the two nations do not lie merely in their geographical positions. Able representatives of one country, residing in the other, have, by their tact, justice and sympathy, tightened the bond of friendship. Of such, the names of Townsend Harris and Judge Bingham, of Mori, Yoshida and Mutsu, are worthy of special tribute.

In the many parks and public places of that beautiful island Empire, there stands no monument to the memory of Perry or Harris, no statue to symbolize the comity of America and Japan. But in the breast of every Japanese is implanted a deep feeling of good-will to America, and it is literally true that to be an American is to be loved and respected. In the absence of a Bartholdi statue, therefore, Columbia might well say with Cato: "I would much rather be asked why I do not have one than why I have one."

Extradition Treaty.

The latest act of diplomatic importance is the extradition treaty of April 29, 1886.

A San Francisco forger fled to Japan and, at the request of the State authorities of California, was delivered up by Japan, even in the absence of any treaty. This occasion gave rise to the suggestion of the extradition treaty, which was soon after concluded. The list of crimes for which extradition may be asked, is comprehensive, and is defined as follows:

---

[1] Young, *Around the World with Gen. Grant*, II, 603.

I. Murder and assault with intent to commit murder.

II. Counterfeiting or altering money, or issuing or bringing into circulation counterfeit or altered money; counterfeiting certificates or coupons of public indebtedness, bank notes, or other instruments of public credit of either of the parties, and the issue or circulation of the same.

III. Forgery or altering and issuing what is forged or altered.

IV. Embezzlement or criminal malversation of the public funds, committed within the jurisdiction of either party by public officers or depositaries.

V. Robbery.

VI. Burglary.

VII. The act of entering, or of breaking and entering, an office of the Government or public authorities, or the offices of banks, trust companies, insurance or other companies, with the intent to commit felony therein.

VIII. Perjury or subornation of perjury.

IX. Rape.

X. Arson.

XI. Piracy by the law of nations.

XII. Murder, assault with intent to kill, and manslaughter, committed on the high seas, on board a ship bearing the flag of the demanding country.

XIII. Malicious destruction of, or attempt to destroy, railways, trams, vessels, bridges, dwellings, public edifices, or other buildings, when the act injures human life.

If the person demanded be held for trial in the country on which the demand is made, it shall be optional with the latter to grant the extradition or to proceed with the trial, provided that, unless the trial be for the crimes for which the fugitive is claimed, the delay shall not prevent ultimate extradition. If it be made to appear that extradition is sought with a view to trial or punishment for a political offence, the surrender shall not take place; nor shall any person surrendered be tried or punished for a political offence committed prior to his extradition, or for any offense other than that in respect of which extradition is granted. Neither of the contracting parties shall be bound to deliver up its own citizens or subjects under the stipulations of this convention, but they shall have power to deliver them if deemed proper.

Treaty Revision.

We have had a glimpse of the social and political condition of Old Japan, when she entered into treaty relations with Western Powers. The ancient régime of duarchy and feudalism needs only to be mentioned, in order to be recollected. Hence, whatever clause in the treaty we may now look upon as unjust, might then have been perfectly legitimate and wise. But Old Japan is no more. The brutal rigor of her laws, the grinding severity of her taxation, the tyranny of her petty princes, the suspicion and fear of foreigners (which necessitated correspondingly undesirable clauses in the treaty), have all gone whither the old exclusive system has vanished. The restoration of the Imperial power, the abrogation of the Shogunate in 1868, the abolition of feudalism in 1871, followed by many a sweeping and radical change in law and administration and accompanied by the introduction of western civilization, the political horizon beaming with the full light of the sun of constitutional liberty—all these facts Western Powers should be curious, if no more, carefully to consider; nay, it is their *moral duty* to recognize them, inasmuch as in their treaties they promised so to do. After July, 1872,[1] the treaties, it was stipulated, could be revised by the mutual consent of the contracting parties. It sounds exceedingly fair to speak of mutuality, but it is a virtue not to be found where there are some seventeen contracting parties, especially while avarice and pride remain universal weaknesses of the sons of Adam.

Japan, according to the treaty, has no right to regulate the rate of her own import duties; hence, whereas the average duty on imports into the States is 30 *per cent.*, in Japan it amounts to not more than $4\frac{1}{2}$ *per cent.* Half of the national revenue of the United States is derived from the customs duties, and even in England, which boasts of its free-trade, nearly one third of the annual revenues come from the same

---

[1] See Art. XIII, Harris, Commercial Treaty.

source. In Japan, all the duties she can raise on an annual importation of some 65 million yen of goods (1888), do not contribute more than 1-19th of her revenue. The customs duties amounted to 4 million yen in 1889-90, in a total government revenue of 76 millions. Is it any wonder that the peasantry are heavily laden with a land tax, and that their condition is deplorable?

The complaint due to the treaty, is not merely a financial one. There is an economic evil ensuing from it. New industries, which with a little protection might be encouraged, cannot compete under existing conditions with those of other countries. Not only new industries, but old ones too, have succumbed before the mighty stream of Western imports. Calico and muslin from England have covered our cotton fields with mourning.

Another objectionable clause in the treaty is that which gives to Treaty Powers the right of extra-territoriality. This insult to the sovereign rights of an independent state was not an insult, so long as our laws remained what they were when the treaty was signed; but, since that time, the codification and administration of our laws have entirely changed.

Not only is extra-territorial concession an injustice to our nation, but also a matter of dissatisfaction to Treaty Powers, since, in the consular courts, the persons (consuls) who sit as judges, as a rule, do not possess the legal training required in the cases coming before them.[1]

The clause in the treaty, according to which foreigners are not allowed to travel beyond certain limits without passports, or to reside without special permission, is but a feeble check

---

[1] Cf. Pres't Angell in *Bibliotheca Sacra*, Jan., 1885. See also a learned dissertation on the *Consular Jurisdiction in Japan*, by Sir Travers Twiss, read before the Association for the Reform and Codification of the Law of Nations, held in Cologne, 1880.—Some six years ago, a foreign young lady (was she not an American?) was guilty of stealing a little trinket in a Japanese store in Yokohama. The case was taken before the consul of her nation for decision. The learned judge, perhaps better trained in psy-

to unconscientious foreigners, who, conscious that they are not under Japanese laws, may do what their cunning may devise.

Odious, doubtless, is the trammel upon free movement to such foreigners as pursue scientific investigations (geologists, etc.) and to missionaries.

All these fetters upon the free exercise of the sovereign rights of an independent State, and upon its free economic development, were put upon Japan when she was an inexperienced novice in foreign intercourse. Now she feels that she has outlived the time when her laws did violence to humanity, when she could not move of herself, on her own responsibility. She feels indeed, at every step of her progress, the dragging weight of the shackles which bind her feet.

Time and again has the attention of the government been turned to the revision of the treaty. The Iwakura Embassy of 1871 had that in view, but the many questions relating to internal improvements and peace engrossed the attention of the government, and, until 1881, the subject was scarcely touched upon. Since that year, it has gravely entered into the field of practical politics. Conference after conference has been held between the foreign representatives and our government, and each time the United States has expressed its satisfaction with the articles contemplated in the revision of the treaty. Even as early as 1878 did the United States government take the initiative step of revising certain portions of the commercial treaties. The convention signed that year (July 25) and ratified the next (April 8), recognized the exclusive right of Japan to adjust its tariff and taxes. But the provision in the last article made the whole convention

---

chology than in justice, declared the fair culprit "not guilty;" that the so-called theft was but a form of kleptomania, for which she was not, of course, responsible. A Daniel come to judgment! All that the poor jeweller could do, was to caution his fellow merchants by hanging a large placard in front of his store, with the statement that "among the late arrivals from abroad, a germ of a most dangerous disease is detected," etc., etc.

inoperative. It said that this convention shall take effect when Japan shall have concluded similar conventions with other Treaty Powers. If, thus, this convention accomplished no practical good, it at least showed America's readiness to comply with the demands of Japan. But the seventeen Powers that have voice in the conference, could not unanimously agree upon every particular. Especially has extra-territoriality been the bone of contention, and to this diplomatic coöperation has added a serious difficulty. Even the representatives of second and third-rate Powers, the number of whose compatriots resident in Japan could almost be counted on the fingers, and the commercial interests of whose country in Japan amounted to a mere paltry sum, felt called upon to deliver long discourses in the conferences of 1886–87. The conditions under which alone the Treaty Powers would accept the revision, formed such a tangled web of guarantees, that they could scarcely be regarded as an improvement on the old terms.

And yet, throughout all these intricacies—nay, even insults, imposed by the European Powers upon Japan, she has never swerved, to borrow the words of a recent writer in the *Edinburgh Review*,[1] "from her obligations, and the result has been that, in nine cases out of ten, the disputes which have agitated the diplomatic world at Yedo, have ended in moral victories to the Japanese."

Count Enouye, the then Minister of Foreign Affairs, was obliged to give up his portfolio in the summer of 1887, and was succeeded by Count Okuma, the special feature of whose policy consisted in revising the treaty with each nation separately. As to the points at issue, Okuma's proposals were scarcely different from Enouye's. The raising of the rate of import duties to some 12 per cent., for twelve years (after which Japan should enjoy perfect tariff-autonomy), and the character of the mixed court (which required that some four

---

[1] *Progress in Japan* in *Edinburgh Review*, July, 1889, p. 52.

foreign judges should sit in the Supreme Court in all appeals made by foreigners) were the main points of consideration.

Okuma's negotiations, however, went a little further than those of his predecessor in office; but his success was not a little due to the times—to these, rather than to his intrinsic diplomatic skill. Likewise, his failure is to be attributed more to the circumstances of the hour than to the defects inherent in his projects. When Okuma had succeeded in obtaining the consent of America, Germany, France and Russia, and was pursuing his policy still further with energy and zeal, he became a victim to the fanaticism of an over-patriotic youth, who succeeded in wounding him so severely that he subsequently resigned his office. The fanaticism of this would-be assassin was but the expression of a wide-spread feeling among certain political factions, who saw in the Judges-guarantee clause of the proposed treaty, a direct violation of the recently adopted Imperial Constitution,[1] which they interpreted to declare that natives alone shall be eligible for the civil service. Added to this was the fear, aroused with amazing suddenness among the more sedate and thinking part of the community, that, should foreigners be granted liberty to travel and settle wheresoever they would, their financial superiority and greater business capacity would lead to disastrous economic and social results. Some went so far as to alarm the public with the idea that an influx of foreigners might immediately follow the unconditional opening of the country; that these, because of the larger scope of their physical and mental powers, might virtually reduce the Japanese to a condition of semi-thraldom. These apprehensions by no means subsided upon the resignation of Okuma; they still continue to make the timid more fearful and, in consequence, reluctant to see an unreserved admission of foreigners, while, at the same time,

---

[1] Art. XIX: "Japanese subjects may, according to qualifications determined in laws or ordinances, be appointed to civil, or military, or any other public offices equally."

the proud are unwilling to submit to the jurisdiction of foreigners in their courts. Since these two conditions are inextricably intermingled, the subject of treaty revision remains a most vexed problem. Such a solution of this problem as may be satisfactory to all parties concerned, is the stupendous task which rests upon the new Minister of Foreign Affairs—Viscount Aoki. Naturally his steps are watched with the greatest interest, if not anxiety, both on the part of Treaty Powers and of Japanese subjects. But of this we may feel assured; whatever proposals our government may make, so long as they are within the bounds of reason and justice, the United States will accede to its desires, with the spirit of fairplay which has ever characterized America's policy in the East. She was the first to set an example in these matters of tariff regulations and extra-territorial rights; but, from the first, an uneasy conscience made her hope for the dawning of a better day, and juster terms, for the struggling though aspiring Island Empire.

Townsend Harris, who was chiefly responsible for the insertion of these clauses into the treaty, confessed more than once, that he did so against his conscience and sense of justice.[1] Little did he dream that the revision would be so long postponed. "The provision giving the right of extra-territoriality to all Americans in Japan," says Harris,[2] "was against my conscience. In a conversation with Governor Macy, the Secretary of State, in 1856, he (Gov. Macy) strongly condemned it as an unjust interference with the municipal law of a country, which no western nation could tolerate for a moment; but he said it would be impossible to have a treaty with any oriental nation, unless it contained that provision. The example of our treaties with Turkey, Persia and the Barbary Powers gave precedents that the Senate would not overlook. I fear I shall

---

[1] See Harris' letters to Mr. House, in the latter's article in the *Atlantic Monthly*, May, 1881.
[2] *Tokio Times*, July 21, 1872.

not live to see this unjust provision abrogated." Harris died in 1878, and "time has changed; but the question remains," as though to mock the memory of its author.

That the government of the United States and its worthy representatives in Japan, have always been ready to undo the work which its first envoy began, has been noted above. Nothing so well illustrates the attitude of America in this matter as the fact, that when, in December, 1888, the proposals for the revision of the treaty were communicated to the Representatives of the Great Powers in Tokyo, the American minister obtained by telegraph, within forty-eight hours, the permission of his government to accept them.

No less interested in the cause of Revision are the American people.[1] Truly, as says Mr. Bryce, "whenever humanity comes into question, the heart of the people is sound."

A straw shows the direction of the wind, and the following extract from a letter by a private person in Cambridge, who, indeed, takes no active part in the politics of the day, will serve to show how warm and true to her interests are the thoughts and heartfelt desires of such Americans as have taken the pains to hear and know the just claims of Japan. The letter reads thus:

"An article by E. H. House, published in the May number of the *Atlantic Monthly*, in 1881, first revealed to me the political and financial condition of Japan and its cause. I was most deeply and painfully impressed by it, and grieved and indignant, too, that my country, having been the *first cause* of Japan's most cruel wrongs, should have allowed those wrongs to go so long unredressed. And I felt that, thereby, America had done herself, as well as Japan who trusted her, a great injustice. But I was but a woman, and what could I do? I would what I could. . . . And so I wrote a most earnest appeal, urging him (President Cleveland) for the sake of justice to ourselves as well as to Japan,

---

[1] See Memorial of American Residents in Japan, March, 1882, in *Senate Miscel. Doc.*, 47th Congress, 1st Session.

to consider her just desires in Treaty Revision; and to act in the matter. . . . Imagine my joy on receiving a prompt acknowledgment from the President, through his private secretary, saying that my letter had been read and referred to the Secretary of State. Some months later I received a long letter from Secretary Bayard and a copy of the Revision of 1878. . . . I am sure that justice will yet be done Japan; and I hope and think within a short time."[1]

Even among the small circle of the author's personal friends, similar expressions of sympathy for Japan and indignation at the unchristian conduct of the Treaty Powers, have been often and warmly expressed. But, that this cause may not be thought to be a matter of mere sentimentality among novices in political matters, we will end with a few words from the pen of one of the greatest living publicists of Europe:

"The old limits which we had given to the idea of the Orient have vanished. East Asia has entered the horizon of Europe. . . . A reconstruction of the Consular system, at least for the most advanced of these lands, Japan, has become necessary and therefore inevitable."[2]

---

[1] The author of this letter is Miss M. Josephine Low, of Cambridge, Mass. The quotation is an extract from her letter to the author, which she wrote in reply to the question how her interest in the Treaty Revision was aroused.

[2] Prof. Dr. Lorenz von Stein, Oesterreichische Monatschrift, January and February, 1884.

CHAPTER IV.

AMERICANS AND AMERICAN INFLUENCES IN JAPAN.

Foreign Influences.

Scarcely any subject requires more delicate handling than that of the influence of one nation upon another. In questions of this sort, there is sure to be an active party to exaggerate, and a passive party to undervalue, a certain given fact. Guizot regards France as a focus of European civilization; Buckle claims a similar honor for England and Heeren for Germany. Admirers of Hellenic culture would discover no trace of oriental influences in it, while the more candid confess their presence. The precept "Honor to whom honor is due," is rarely remembered in the enthusiasm, the prejudice and pride of nationalities and races. Some Europeans and Americans seem to entertain the notion, that the recent changes in Japan are exclusively due to her intercourse with their countries, and her very name "Japan" as being bestowed by Europeans on account of her production of lacquer! This is a grievous mistake, and is fraught with more grievous inferences. Sure enough, the most conservative of the Japanese cannot deny the great debt which his country owes to foreign influences; but no alien nation can claim the honor of being the originator of the political and social movements which lifted Japan from the thraldom of her traditions, and made her a new nation on the face of the globe. Well says a New

England divine,[1] "As it would be vain to attempt to comprehend our late civil war by beginning at Sumter, or even with the Compromise measures of 1851; so one will be misled, who, in attempting to understand the Japan of to-day, looks only at events since Perry's time."

A candid observer must admit, however, that the Revolution of 1868, as well as the changes incidental to it, was hastened by the presence of Foreign Powers. He must also admit that, were it not for this presence, the solidarity of the nation would not have been completed so soon; neither would the centralization of Imperial power have been accomplished with such facility. The influence of foreigners at first, therefore, may be likened to a "catalytic action" in chemical reactions, or perhaps, more appropriately, to the action of a solid substance which, in virtue of its mere presence, effects the crystalization of a fluid. Innumerable instances of this kind can be cited in the histories of European states. But, besides these general, indirect and involuntary influences, there were definite impressions which the United States made upon Japan from the earliest days of their friendship.

Beginning with Perry,

we might consider how he and his staff impressed our people. First of all, he gave the idea, lately found so false, that America was a great naval power. His stately fleet was an object lesson teaching this. To a people with whom war was the noblest vocation (as yet the most advanced nation is not free from this taint of barbarism), and among whom military virtues were esteemed the highest, a show of martial power was most impressive, and Perry gave a heroic impression of his countrymen. "Americans," he said, "are people of few words, and they always mean what they say." As he did not take with him the *Congressional Globe* to verify the contrary, he made good his word by his reserved demeanor.

---
[1] Griffis, *Mikado's Empire*, 296.

The President's letter to the Emperor, originally written by Daniel Webster, was exceedingly simple in phraseology, concise in statement and good-natured in tone. Its very simplicity was supplemented by the gravity of its bearer; its conciseness was emphasized by his taciturnity; and to its good-nature his bold courage forbade familiar approach. But the official reserve of both the Japanese commissioners and the Americans, lost much of its rigidity in the banquets held at the conclusion of the convention. The words of a wine-bibber at one of these feasts—"Japan and America, all the same heart"—uttered as he threw his arm around the Commodore's neck, express the conviviality which volumes of diplomatic correspondence do not publish.

If the personal intercourse of the parties was thus agreeable, no less attractive were the presents of the United States government. Unfortunately, liquors and wines formed a considerable bulk of these presents; but they were by no means the principal offerings. Swords, rifles, muskets and pistols were included. A telescope, clocks and books of various kinds, formed a valuable part. Agricultural implements and eight baskets of potatoes were no doubt symbolical of "Columbia's virgin soil." But, by far the most important of the presents were the telegraph instruments and a complete model of a small railway train, although Dr. Williams says the corn-cracker and rice-huller were more popular. The telegraphic apparatus was set in working order, to the great delight and amazement of the on-lookers. A circular railroad was built, and the locomotive whirled round and round at the rate of twenty miles an hour. The childish wonder with which the spectators of Stephenson's first locomotive gaped at its motion (so graphically described by Miss Kemble at the time), could be seen in the countenance of every Japanese beholder. Perhaps no two exponents of Western civilization could be better selected than the telegraph and the locomotive. On account of that taciturnity which characterized the diplomats, we are kept in the dark as to the depth of the impressions then made upon the Japanese commissioners. But, if their subsequent actions give any clue to their thoughts, it is but just to infer, that no longer did they look upon those who could make and manage such engines as "barbarians."

Speaking of the peaceful manner in which the American influences in Japan were inaugurated, Dr. Samuel Wells Williams, who was a secretary to Perry, writes: "Not a shot has been fired, not a man wounded, not a piece of property destroyed, not a boat sunk or a single Japanese to be found who is the worse off, so far as we know, for the visit of the 'American expedition.' Its ultimate results can only be estimated when time has properly disclosed them both in respect of trade between the two countries and intercourse between their peoples; but, in the higher benefits likely to flow to the Japanese by their introduction into the family of civilized nations, I see a hundred fold return for all the expenses of this expedition to the American Government."[1]

The conquest of peace which Perry thus inaugurated, Harris carried further.

Townsend Harris in Yedo.

The significance of the step which Harris took in leaving the confines of Shimoda to visit the Yedo court, in 1857, is best shown in the official notifications of that time. One of these addressed to officials reads:[2]

"The present audience of the American Ambassador will be a precedent for all foreign countries, and must, therefore, be attended to with the greatest care. As intercourse with foreign countries necessitates the *repeal of old regulations and restrictions*, the matter is attended with difficulty, and the *possible evils cannot be fore-*

---

[1] See *Life and Letters of Samuel Wells Williams*, by his son, N. Y. and Lond., 1889.

[2] Minute and interesting details of T. Harris' visit are to be found in *Foreign Relations*, 1879-80, Vol. I, 622 sq., translated from Japanese account.

8

seen; you must therefore neglect nothing, but attend to all things with the greatest care, as the Tycoon's order requires."

Twenty days later (September), another paternal notice appears from the Government:

" When in a short time the American ambassador visits Yedo, it will not be necessary to repair the *Yashikis* (residences of princes) along the road; the temporary boards may be left as they are. Each householder is to keep his portion of the road swept clean. It will, likewise, not be necessary to set out the ornamented firemen's baskets before the houses, nor to place guards there. Travellers may be allowed to pass along as usual. Guards should be placed at the small stations or guard-houses, to suppress any disorder, if required to do so by the officers in attendance on the ambassador. Beggars must be removed out of the way. As to sight-seers, they may stand at designated spots along the road, but they are not allowed to crowd together at the upper story windows of tenement houses and like places. As much as possible, all encounters of persons on horseback are to be avoided. Great care must be taken by officials to avoid all noise and confusion on the way," etc., etc.

If any comment on the above extracts is necessary, it is sufficient to state that the former evidently contains a germ of political changes, and the latter of social reforms—and these as the American representative passes by!

In his interview with the governor of foreign affairs, Harris dwelt particularly on three points: first, the Monroe doctrine of his country, obliquely condemning the French and the English policy in China and making clear America's immunity from the blood of the Opium War; secondly, the religious freedom in his country, divesting the governor of any fear in the direction of religious aggression; lastly, the usefulness of mutual trade.[1]

---

[1] For the British view of Harris' actions, see Alcock, *Three Years in Japan*, N. Y., 1863.

By his tact and talent, Harris gained the entire confidence of the Shogunate, so much so that when, after years of residence in Japan, he was about to leave the country, a formal letter was addressed by the Japanese authorities to the Secretary of State, asking that his stay might be prolonged. His conduct through the trying moments of the nation, just in the throes of a new birth, cannot be too highly praised. If "an ambassador," according to Wotton's definition, " is an honest man sent to lie abroad for the commonwealth," Harris was no diplomat. If, on the contrary, an American minister to an Oriental Court is a representative of the moral principles of the great Christian Republic, Harris deserves the name in its best sense.

Harris and Perry Compared.

Mild as were Perry's persuasions, his conduct was audacious. Townsend Harris also spoke in gentle terms and his conduct was equally gentle. Perry's word was backed by a powerful display; not so was that of Harris. The former was brought up a warrior from his youth, and, as a warrior, he knew how to deal with other races ; the latter was trained as a merchant, and as such he gained knowledge of different peoples. The one was a soldier-diplomat, and diplomacy was with him tactics ; the other was a man of peace, and diplomacy was his tact.[1] The mission of Perry was that of a pioneer; that of Harris of a sower. The duty of one was to force a barred door open ; that of the other was to keep it so. Perry was

---

[1] Of Perry, Dr. Williams writes: "As to the real views of the U. S. Government or the plans of Com. Perry, I have less confidence since I have seen more of his character ; the previous experience of victory in Mexico may strengthen his determination to drive by force matters which can be attained only by long and patient treating." *Life and Letters*, 198. Of Harris, he writes: "I have seen a good deal of Townsend Harris since he came up to Shanghai, and should judge from his conversation that he is truly a Christian man. His success is better explained if the fact be known that it was in answer to prayer." p. 205.

dissuaded by his government from resorting to warlike measures, when he had planned them, while Harris dissuaded it from using such, when he was instructed to plan them. Perry inspired awe rather than confidence; Harris, confidence rather than awe. Both were good, faithful servants and as such deserve appropriate praise and appreciation.

Sufficient justice is not yet done to the memory of Townsend Harris. Perry is fortunate in having a recent biographer in his admirer; but the candle of Harris is still kept under a bushel. A monument to the memory of Perry stands in the Touro Park, in Newport, R. I.; a portrait of Harris, hanging in the hall of the College of the City of New York, is the only means by which the city of his adoption attests its appreciation of the man—and this in no connection with his service in Japan. Even in Japan, how rarely is the name of Harris mentioned! The expedition of Perry was heralded with a loud blare of trumpets, while the coming of Harris was attended with no demonstration. Four thick quarto volumes made known to the world the minutest details of Perry's expedition, while Harris even forbade the publication of his papers, until twenty-five years after his decease.[1]

Thus has it always been. An oak falls noisily crashing through the forest; the acorns drop with scarce a sound. To generations after, the acorns prove the greater blessing. Men have not yet learned what conquests there are in peace and in silence.

Educational Influence.

"If the tutorship of the United States in Japan is to be successful, it must be based on deeper and broader principles of philanthropy than have heretofore been practised in the intercourse of nations—a philanthropy which shall recognize

---

[1] In his letter to the writer, General George W. Cullum, who was an intimate friend of T. H., says that the papers referred to are deposited in the Historical Society, N. Y., and with the condition mentioned above.

not merely the distinction of strength and power between nations, but the duties of magnanimity, moderation and humanity—a philanthrophy which shall not be content with sending armies and navies to compel, but which shall send teachers to instruct and establish schools on the American system, where philosophy and morals as well as religious faith are taught with just regard to their influences in their social and domestic life."[1] These words of one of America's greatest statesmen have been literally fulfilled.

The first educational work of the Americans in Japan was necessarily confined to imparting the English language. We have seen that the young McDonald, in 1848, improved the hours of his captivity by teaching the "American language." At the time Perry and Harris came, Dutch was the medium of diplomacy. There were scarcely any who could understand a dozen English words in succession. Mr. Spalding says, that among the many presents Perry brought, *Webster's Dictionary* was perhaps the one most valued. The want of English interpreters was so severely felt, that anybody who could mutter a few English words or who could spell out A-S-I-A, was employed at a high remuneration. Schools, private and public, arose for instruction in English. Of the latter, one was the nucleus of the present Imperial University; of the former, Mr. Fukuzawa's School, established in a humble manner in 1868, and growing with the growth of western knowledge, has been the cradle of many bright intellects and is still an object of Japanese pride. In those days, the demand for foreign teachers was so great, that clerks in American houses left their counters and hastened to the school-room to teach writing, while sailors put aside their blouses to assume the dignity of imparting what little knowledge they possessed in the three Rs. Freely enough did they swear, unmindful of the difficulty their scholars had with dictionaries, in trying to

---

[1] Seward's *Travels*, p. 98.

find the significance of profane words. The pipes with which they regaled their hours of recess, were scrutinized by the boys with respect and admiration for their tremendous size. If it had not been for the missionaries, these impostors of learning would have reaped far more honor and recompense than they did. In government institutions, these impositions were of course at their minimum.

Early in 1872, when Arinori Mori was Chargé d'affaires at Washington, he sent circulars of inquiry to prominent American educators—among them Theodore D. Woolsey, William A. Stearns, Peter Cooper, Octavius Perinchief, Mark Hopkins, Julius H. Seelye, James McCosh, Joseph Henry, David Murray, B. G. Northrop, Charles W. Eliot, George S. Boutwell and John A. Gainfield. The answers to the circulars, giving a general and comprehensive view of the effect of education upon the well-being of nations, and making suggestions for an educational system for Japan, were published, in 1873, for the benefit of Japanese readers, appearing in book-form, under the title of *Education in Japan*.

One can hardly realize the rapidity with which western knowledge was disseminated in Japan. When one takes up a paper and sees how extensively and freely—and, indeed, too confidently—Spencer, Huxley, Buckle and J. S. Mill are quoted from the original, he can scarcely believe, that, not more than twenty years ago, *Webster's Spelling-Books* were so few that an assiduous student had to copy A B C's, and one who could expound old *Peter Parley*, was thought a well-read man. In those days, *Wilson's Readers*, *Pinneo's Grammar*, *Mitchell's Geography*, were the universal text-books. *Quackenbos' Natural History* and *United States History* and *Goodrich's* Historical series, formed a higher grade of class-books. The introduction of *Wayland's Moral Science* and *Political Economy*, formed quite an epoch in the educational progress of young Japan. *Sander's Union Readers*, *Brown's Grammar*, *Guyot's* and *Murray's* Geographical Series, *Gray's Botany*, *Morse's Zoology*, *Youmans'*, *Hitchcock's*, *Jarvis'* and

Cutter's Physiology, *Robinson's* Mathematical Series, *Perry's* and *Walker's* Political Economies, *Haven's* Mental Philosophy, *Porter's* Human Intellect, *Swinton's* History, are now standard text-books in many schools throughout the Empire. For works of high authority, we turn more to England, France and Germany. A few American writers much read and more quoted among the Japanese, are *Carey* (Social Science), *Woolsey* (International Law and Political Science) and *Draper* (Conflict of Science and Religion, and Intellectual Development of Europe). *Hodge, Barnes, Joseph Cook, Whedon, McCosh* (counting him as an American), *Beecher, Talmage* and *McIlvaine*, represent American theological thought. To literature, busy young Japan has not paid due attention, but of the few authors who are read, *Emerson, Longfellow, Professor Matthews* and *Washington Irving*, are most liked.

That the early educational influences of new Japan were almost exclusively American, is due to several causes. Education received the first attention of the government after the Restoration, and naturally Japan turned to the United States, as she first opened the country, and as her representatives were agreeable and helpful in carrying out, perhaps unbeknown to themselves, the philanthropic ideas of Mr. Seward. To Mr. Arinori Mori, for a long time identified with western civilization in Japan and late Minister of Education, may be attributed, in great measure, the introduction of American influences. Among the people, Mr. Fukuzawa, long an exponent of western ideas, has always been an admirer of America. The presence of many Americans as missionaries or otherwise, also contributed to the fact above represented.

Immediately after the Kai-Sei-Gakko (the nucleus of the present imperial University) was founded, the service of GUIDO F. VERBECK, D. D., was secured as President, 1869. Dr. Verbeck was one of the first missionaries from the United States, whence he came to Japan in 1859, and is still an untiring worker in the field. Notwithstanding the government's dislike to Christianity, his wide accomplishments were duly appreciated, and he was engaged by it in more than one capacity. When his presidency of the University terminated in 1873, he was awarded the decoration of the third order of merit by the Emperor. Dr. Verbeck has written several religious tracts, as well as memorials to the Japanese government, and he has also been on the committee for the translation of the Bible into Japanese.

DAVID MURRAY, LL. D., long Secretary of the Board of Regents of the University of the State of New York, Albany, was invited by the Japanese government, in 1873, to act as Adviser to the Department of Education. He rendered valuable service in helping to carry out the elementary school system, an outline of which had been formed before his arrival. Dr. Murray remained in Japan for six years, during which time the educational museums were completed under his supervision. At the termination of his engagement, he was honored with the decoration of the Order of the Rising Sun.

The Normal school, opened in 1872 and followed two years later by one for women, has been the work of a Kentucky gentleman, M. M. SCOTT, A. M., now the Head Master of the largest school in Honolulu. An excellent teacher himself, he introduced the normal school system, which does credit to its framer as well as to his country; for, while the university, planned at first after the American and English models, is now greatly modified by Prussian influences, and while the elementary educational regulations, formerly adopted from the United States, are now more German and Belgian in their character, the normal school system alone may still be said to be essentially American in character.

Musical education received no small impetus from MR. LUTHER W. MASON. As he was for seventeen years a successful teacher of music in Boston and has a high reputation in his department, the Japanese government was desirous of securing his services for the introduction of foreign music, which, in conjunction with the Japanese, has formed a part of the elementary school curriculum since

1871. He came to Japan in 1879, and, during his engagement of three years, rendered signal service in improving the native music and in harmonizing it with the European.

For instructions in gymnastic exercises, DR. LELAND, a graduate of Amherst College, now of Boston, was in the Japanese employ for some years.

The training of nurses, a new and important departure in the education of Japanese women, was placed for a while under the charge of MISS LINDA R. RICHARDS, at one time Superintendent of the Boston City Hospital.

CAPTAIN L. L. JANES was invited, in 1871, to found a military school in Kumamoto. The plan of the school was changed from a military to a civil basis, and Captain Janes, during his stay of five years, was actively helpful in many ways, pedagogical, industrial and religious.

Numberless institutions have been founded for the education of girls, from the rudimentary "ragged schools" up to colleges; by government, private individuals and by foreign missions. Those under government supervision are sadly devoid of religious influences; those undertaken by private effort are inefficient in proper appliances, and those under the management of foreign missionary societies, while they supply the defects of the other two, are often denationalizing in their tendency.

GENERAL KURODA, when he visited the United States for the first time, was struck by the intelligence and freedom of American women; and on his return he urged the importance of female education. Many American ladies have been in the employ of government as well as private schools. Begun in a small way by MRS. DR. J. C. HEPBURN, in 1867, missionary activity in the education of our women has been of steady growth, and counts among its promoters many a self-sacrificing "handmaid of the Lord." Scarcely any field is more open to American usefulness and more promising than this. Of seventy-four foreign ladies connected with protestant missions, early in 1887, sixty-seven were from the United States, and most of them engaged in teaching.

In pedagogical authorship, DR. HEPBURN's *Japanese-English and English-Japanese Dictionary* stands the highest in usefulness. It has passed through several editions. DR. S. R. BROWN's *Prendergast's Mastery System* applied to Japanese (1875), has been helpful to beginners. PROFESSOR TERRY's *Elements of Law* was intended especially for his students in the Imperial University. DR. J. C. CUTTER's *Anatomy and Physiology* came out in Philadelphia, while he was a professor in Sapporo. DR. W. E. GRIFFIS is the author of a series of *Readers* for Japanese beginners. DR. EASTLAKE has labored with untiring energy in every way practicable, to encourage the study of the English language in Japan.

In art, Japan has learned little from the United States, nor is there any prospect of learning much from them in the near future. But from an American it received an invaluable suggestion; namely, that of the revival of ancient Japanese pictorial art and of eventually creating a definite Japanese school. The idea originated with DR. ERNST FENOLLOSA, for some time Professor of Philosophy in the Imperial University. Not a little had he to contend with in maintaining his ground against young radical artists, who would foolishly have everything western, as well as against old-fashioned painters, who felt their sanctuary molested by an alien intruder. The merits of Prof. Fenollosa's views were fully appreciated by the government, and, under appointment as Commissioner of Arts, he has visited Europe and America, to inspect the management of art-schools and museums, and to purchase books and art-reproductions for the Imperial government. Mr. Fenollosa's ideas have not yet borne their full fruit, but, if any prediction of their success is possible, his work will prove a pioneer step in the development of more solid, healthy, national ideas and self-respect, which must and will supplant the present indiscriminate adoption of Occidental thoughts and things.

Let it be noticed in passing, that some of the characters in American history have become to the Japanese familiar illustrations in morals. The perseverance of Columbus, the "pluck" of Captain John Smith, the gentleness of Pocahontas, the endurance of the Pilgrim Fathers, the virtues of Washington, the good sense of Franklin, the sturdy manhood and integrity of Lincoln, are oft-quoted examples.

Scientific Services.

Closely allied to the subject of education, and, indeed, in many cases forming a part of it, is that of the scientific service rendered by American specialists in or for Japan.

PROFESSOR RAPHAEL PUMPELLY, formerly of Harvard, was engaged in 1861 by the Shogunal government, together with MR. WILLIAM P. BLAKE, for the purpose of mineralogical explorations. When they arrived in Japan, the government (remember that 1861 was one of those anti-foreign years), having met with much opposition in regard to admitting foreigners to many points in the main island, these gentlemen were sent to Hokkaido (Yesso), to examine certain mines and prospects, and to give instruction in mining and metallurgy. There they remained two years. Professor Pumpelly's activity, and hence his usefulness, was greatly reduced on account of the political condition of the country; but he succeeded in introducing the use of powder and blasting in mines and quarries. His scientific observations were published in the Smithsonian Contributions of 1867, and his personal narrative in "Across America and Asia."

BENJAMIN SMITH LYMAN, now of the State Geological Survey of Pennsylvania, was in the employ of the Japanese government for eight years, 1873-80 inclusive. For three years under the Colonial Department, as a member of General Capron's staff, he worked in the geological survey of

Hokkaido, the report on which formed a valuable contribution to the development of that island. At the expiration of the term, his service was secured by the Home Department for the survey of oil lands. The remainder of his stay was devoted to superintending the completion of the maps and the work of the survey for the Public Works Department. Among the colleagues of Mr. Lyman, were Messrs. H. S. MUNROE and WASSON.

DR. ANTISELL, now of the Patent Office in Washington, went out as a chemist, with General Capron, but, after a year and a half's work with him, he was transferred to the Paper Money Bureau, where his chief service consisted in the preparation of inks for the currency.

PROFESSOR EDWARD SYLVESTER MORSE, whom we shall again consider as a writer on Japan, visited the country in the summer of 1877, for the purpose of studying marine zoölogy, especially the embryology of the Brachiopods. During his sojourn, he was offered the professorship of Zoölogy in the Imperial University, with a contract for two years. A part of this time he spent in the United States, fulfilling his lecturing engagements. On his return to his post of duty, he improved the Zoölogical Museum by his own collections, and exchanged specimens with Harvard, Yale, etc. He also formed an Archæological Museum for the University. After the term of the contract was over, he returned to his home in Salem, Mass. In 1882, he made his third visit to Japan, when he devoted most of his time to collecting material for his work on "Japanese Homes," and for a forthcoming work on Japanese pottery. The latter is the outcome of an important discovery he made in Omori, near Tokyo. During his first visit to Japan, while passing through this place, he observed that a railway cut had been made through a shell-heap, precisely like those along the shores of New England, and on the Baltic coast. On examining it carefully, he found traces of an ancient race, which had, in his opinion, preceded even the Ainos.

Professor Morse was succeeded in his professorship by Mr. C. O. WHITMAN, at present of the Biological Laboratory, Milwaukee, Wis. His instruction was confined mainly to Embryology and Comparative Anatomy. The aim of his work during the two years of his stay, was to make original investigators, and among his pupils were some who have since distinguished themselves in their special lines in German universities. Professor Whitman published a pamphlet on "Zoölogy in the University of Tokio," in 1881. His studies of the leeches of Japan appear in the Quarterly Journal of Microscopic Science, London.

PROFESSOR H. M. PAUL, now Assistant Astronomer at the U. S. N. Observatory, filled the chair of Astronomy in the Imperial University for three years, beginning in 1880. His time was occupied in teaching astronomy, the theory of probability and of "least squares."

PROFESSOR T. C. MENDENHALL, for some time of the Meteorological Department in Washington, now in charge of the U. S. Coast Survey, the author of "A Century of Electricity," filled for three years (1878–'81) the chair of Experimental Physics in the University. He also organized and took charge of a meteorological observatory. Of his purely scientific works in Japan may be enumerated, among others, the memoirs on the force of gravity at Tokyo and on the summit of Fujiyama, on the wave length of the principal Fraunhofer lines of the solar spectrum, experiments for the determination of velocity of sound, the electric thermometry for underground temperatures, &c.

PROFESSOR WINFIELD SCOTT CHAPLIN, now of Harvard, and MR. J. A. L. WADDELL, now of Kansas City, were both for some years connected with the Imperial University as professors of Civil Engineering. MR. F. F. JEWETT, Professor of Chemistry in Oberlin College, had the chair of Chemistry in the same institution.

In medicine, little that is original has been done by Americans in Japan, if indeed by any foreigner. The Medical Department of the University has been altogether under German influences. But, nevertheless, American doctors have been usefully, though silently, engaged. Almost all of them came to Japan in connection with missions. Among these may be mentioned DR. SIMMONS, a veteran physician in Japan (now deceased), DR. J. C. HEPBURN, a pioneer in missions, DR. JOHN C. BERRY, DR. HARWELL and DR. WALLACE TAYLOR. MRS. BUCKLEY has also been a medical missionary. The different missions have hospitals and dispensaries. If the undenominational Christian Medical School, Hospital and Training School for Nurses, where instruction is to be given through the medium of English and which has been for some years under consideration, should be completed, the enterprise will surely prove a great benefit to Japan and a gain to missionary activity. Among those American physicians in Japan who are independent of any missionary organization, may be mentioned DR. JOHN C. CUTTER,[1] who was for a long time professor of Human Physiology and Veterinary Medicine in Sapporo, and DR. NORTON WILLIS WHITNEY, who is connected with the American Legation and who has in that capacity resided several years in the country.

Postal System.

Until the year 1871, the conveyance of letters was done by means of the primitive system of "hikyaku" (runners). According to this system, it cost 25 cents to send a message for a distance of 150 miles. The absence of better facilities for the exchange of correspondence, made it necessary that the English, French and American governments should take into their own hands the establishment of postoffices in the open ports, for the accommodation of their respective citizens. This continued till 1871, when the postal system on the Western plan was introduced. In the fall of the next year,

---

[1] Since returned to America.

MR. SAMUEL M. BRYAN, now President of a Telephone Company in Washington, D. C., then of the U. S. Post Office, made a journey to Japan on his own responsibility, to offer his services in the improvement and extension of her postal system. Then a comparatively young man without pretensions, Mr. Bryan was naturally not trusted at once. His countryman, E. Peshine Smith, who was then adviser in International Law to the Imperial Government, said that a postal convention could not as yet be legally signed.
After some months' discussion, Mr. Bryan obtained permission to try the experiment of persuading the Treaty Powers to sign such a convention. So delicate an undertaking, like charity, must begin at home; so he returned to the United States, where he signally succeeded in concluding the convention, on the 6th of August, 1873. It was signed by the Postmaster General, Mr. Creswell, and the chargé d'affaires (ad interim) Takaki, was ratified in April, 1874, and went into effect from the beginning of 1875, the detailed regulations for its execution being signed in July, 1874. Soon after (April, 1875), the agreement for the prepayment in full to destination, of the postage on newspapers and other packages of printed matter, patterns and samples of merchandise, was made.
As Special Commissioner of the Japanese Government, Mr. Bryan went to Europe and contracted a promise with England and France, which was only conditional, since they must first see the working of the American Convention, in order to be convinced of the advisability of such a novel step.
For some time after 1875, mails to the United States were transported by the Pacific Mail Steamship Company, free of charge to Japan. The single rate of international letter postage was, in the agreement of February, 1876, reduced from fifteen to five cents.
The efficiency of the new enterprise was soon recognized by other Treaty Powers,[1] and on the 1st of June, 1877, only

---

[1] The British post-offices in Japan closed in the beginning of 1880.

six years after anything like a postal system was attempted, Japan was formally admitted into the General Postal Union. Two years later she joined the International Telegraphic Convention, and, in 1885, was concluded the Money Order Convention with the United States.

Religious Influences.

The history of Protestant missions in Japan has no connection with the Catholic missions of the sixteenth century. If there was any, it was the hostile feeling against Christianity in general, engendered by the latter, which the former had to conquer. Good Christian people explain away any obstacle in evangelistic work, by stretching the doctrine of original sin —"Men love darkness rather than light." While the universality of this truth can never be gainsaid, the animosity of the Japanese against Christianity was also historical and political, hence it was bitterest among the *samurai* class, to whom Buddhism was a dead letter and Shintoism was worthy of respect only as an ancestral legacy.

Since 1859,[1] when the first Protestant missionaries, representing the Episcopal, Presbyterian and Reformed Dutch churches (all of America) arrived, even as late as 1869, and still later, "the swaggering *samurai*, with two swords, cast many a scowling look at the hated foreigners." "When such a subject (Religion)," says an eye-witness, "was mooted in the presence of a Japanese, his hand would almost involuntarily be applied to his throat, to indicate the extreme perilousness of such a topic." Even a native teacher of language could not be had for about a year, and, when one was obtained, he

---

[1] Already in 1858, two American clergymen, the Rev. Mr. Syle and Chaplain Henry Wood, were in Nagasaki on board the *Minnesota*. They and Dr. S. W. Williams wrote to the Directors of the Episcopal, Reformed and Presbyterian Mission Boards, urging them to appoint missionaries to Japan. Within the coming year, agents from these societies were in Shanghai. See *Life and Letters of S. W. Williams*, p. 285.

proved to be a spy. In vain, for some years, did the missionaries distinguish between Protestantism and Catholicism; in vain did they endeavor to allay the fears of the people, by assuring them that their object in coming was not "to swallow up their country." A pamphlet by a Buddhist priest, in 1868, says: "Compared with the Roman Catholic Religion, this (Protestant faith) is a very cunning doctrine; although they try to make out that there is nothing abominable in it, they are really foxes of the same hole, and it is really more injurious than the Roman Catholic doctrine."

The political excitement and commotion, always unfavorable to the spread of religion, during the years from the arrival of Perry to the abolition of Feudalism, was a counter-influence against the progress of missions. It was in view of these facts, that Dr. Guido F. Verbeck, the historian of the Protestant missions in Japan, calls this period—"the period of preparation and promise." The second period, "a season of progressive realization and performance," auspiciously began, in 1873, by the adoption of the Gregorian Calendar in place of the old lunar system, by the removal of public edicts against Christianity, by the return of the Iwakura Embassy, by the commencement of the New Testament translation, by the arrival of a considerable re-enforcement of missionaries. Three years later, a concession was made by the Japanese government to foreigners, and virtually to Christianity, when it decreed, in March, 1876, that Sundays should henceforth be observed as holidays, instead of "one-six," (1st, 6th, 11th, 16th, 21st and 26th days of each month).

At present there are some twenty or more evangelical organizations, exclusive of the native churches, represented in Japan; of these, the largest proportion is from America. They are no longer "like unto children sitting in the markets," piping or mourning unheeded. By dint of perseverance in good work, they have now gained the hearing of both the low and the high. They have become a power in the nation. Despite obstacles, of which indifference and agnosticism are perhaps the greatest, the ultimate conquest of Christianity in one form or another is quite likely.

Indifference to religious truths—to truths which cannot be chopped by a logic-machine—is a deplorable feature of the present generation of our youths. But this state of things will not long continue. To be religious is the nature of man, and if the Japanese will not embrace Religion, it will embrace them.

Agnosticism, likewise, cannot long hold sway. Mental suspension, which is Agnosticism, has in itself no element of continuity. However, so long as its influence is recognized, merely to sneer at it, as many a good missionary is prone to do, is to confess one's inability to counteract its work.

The chief hindrances to evangelical work, however, do not lie in indifference or in Agnosticism, but in the personnel and the *modus operandi* of the missionaries. With all respect for the high motives which may prompt most missionaries to enter the field, it cannot be denied that too many of them are far from being exemplary in their methods of work or in their intellectual equipment. Too often, inexperienced, sanguine young men go forth, exuberant with the hope that, with their meagre store of knowledge and experience, they may be able to convince pagan philosophy of its errors.[1] The result is, that they find their scanty college education inadequate to satisfy the intellectual demands made upon them by the better educated of the natives, and their small spiritual experience insufficient to guide the more consecrated. Naturally, therefore, the field of missionary activity confines itself to the lower strata of society. The missionaries find excuse for this course in pointing to the history of the primitive Church, reminding

---

[1] "With them (Japanese), more, perhaps, than is the case in any other nation in the world, owing to the inborn politeness of the Japanese, religious intercourse, as well as all other, must be carried on, never in the spirit of assumption, but always in that of sympathy. The principle of reciprocity in religion must be observed even more scrupulously than in the realm of trade." Arthur May Knapp's letter in the Boston *Transcript*, Sept. 23, 1889.

us that the Religion of Christ seeks its converts first among the humble and the lowly. They forget, however, that Christ chose the best educated and the most energetic of his disciples for missionary labor among the Gentiles.

Mr. House's delineation of the missionaries as "well-intending but curiously unintelligent and illiterate professors of a narrow and microscopic Christianity," and of their views as "superficial, one-sided and utterly selfish,"[1] is, also, too well grounded to be denied. At the same time, we must remember that Mr. House has, with the pen of an artist and with a definite moral purpose in view, sketched the characters of his Japanese romance in sharper profile than they actually exist. The harsh, repellent character of the Misses Philipson and of Miss Jackman, is no more typical of the band of Christian workers than is the stolid and mercenary Santo typical of Japanese husbands—even of the lower classes.

A sad feature of the mission work, is the very little contact between those foreigners who profess to teach "pure religion and undefiled," and the Japanese. Few can become as a Jew unto the Jews, or as without the law to them that are without law (I Cor., ix, 20-23). "To look down upon the heathen was," as House puts it, "in a great measure, what they had come to the East for." The lack of personal sympathies, interests and communion, and therefore of real spiritual union, between the foreign missionaries and native converts, is a great barrier to the spread of Christianity. Herein lies a cause for Canon Taylor's question whether missions are a success.

Another lamentable fact connected with mission work, is the lack of union among the different denominational representatives, nay, even hostility among them. The sectarian bigots revive on a heathen land their old petty jealousies, for which their forefathers fought and burned one another. Nothing is more ugly and repugnant to Japanese eyes than these sectarian

---

[1] *Yone Santo*, Chap. II.

quarrels and jealousies; worse than that, the Japanese seekers find themselves puzzled by a maze of conflicting teachings of different Christian bodies.

The virtue of self-renunciation—the corner-stone of the Christian Religion—is required, not only of each individual, but of every organization that professes the name of Jesus. " Whosoever would save his life shall lose it; and whosoever shall lose his life for my sake and the gospel's, shall save it " (Mark VIII, 35). Missionary organizations in Japan—and elsewhere—must ever remember that they are human institutions, and must ever be prepared to sacrifice their life for His "sake and the gospel's." Far be it, therefore, from any of them, to try to enforce upon the new souls won to Christ, any peculiarity or fancy of their own small life. The history of the past nineteen centuries should teach us, that, broadly speaking, Christianity, in its progress towards universality, has beautifully adapted itself to different conditions of mankind. The Slavic peoples have their form of the Religion of Jesus; among the Romance nations it has assumed a somewhat modified shape; to the Teutonic mind it presents itself in another light; why, then, should not "this Light, which lighteth every man coming into the world," reveal its rays afresh and understandingly in the Land of the Sun-rise? Why, then, should Aryan messengers of the World's salvation ruthlessly tread upon the institutions and characters of Asia, and, at the same time, force upon it those of their own race—nay, of the old Jewish tribes too? Why introduce to a people indifferent to ritualism, the rite of water baptism? Even the beautiful sacrament of the Eucharist almost deteriorates into a farce, among a people to whom "bread" and "wine" convey no idea of the necessaries of life—physical or spiritual.[1] If the democracy of confession

---

[1] Very significant is a picture of the Last Supper, which is to be seen in one of the stained glass windows of a church in the Westphalian town of Soest. There, the solemn company is represented as sitting around a table, on which is spread, instead of unleavened bread, black rye bread (*Pumper-*

(John xv, 15) is to be taught, why contradict it with priesthood (clergy), which very often means priestcraft and, as such, is allied to many forms of heathenism?

Back to Primitive Christianity! To the simplicity and spirituality of the Church of the Acts let all Christians return. A people newly converted can best do this—"the last shall be first." In one word, the divine religion of Christ, divested of all human wrappings—of sacramentalism, sacerdotalism, sectarianism—alone is welcome. If symbols and institutions must be had, leave them to "the whirring loom of time" to weave; but let them not be "clothed upon." A home-made garment (for are not all institutions, as says the Sage of Chelsea, garments?), if homelier, fits better and lasts longer than the latest style of ready-made clothing.

While thus the work of the missionaries is open to criticism —criticism by those on-lookers who take no active part in it— justice, if nothing else, requires that their labors should be recognised and highly appreciated. In fact the direct and indirect services rendered by missionaries, both as individuals and as a collective body, are not yet rightly estimated or understood; on the contrary, they are often misunderstood and misrepresented. However, sooner or later, the Japanese people, believers or unbelievers, will confess the inestimable benefit which the missions have conferred upon the civilization of their country; the more so when, in a few years, foreigners of every character may settle in the interior of the country. Well does House put these words in the mouth of Dr. Charwell:[1]

"They (missionaries) are useful, extremely useful, in setting a pattern of social cleanliness and decorum, which foreigners

---

nichel), instead of the pascal lamb, a piece of ham, and instead of wine, beer. How much more perfectly these substitutes convey to the minds of Westphalian peasants, whose daily food they are, Christ's meaning of the symbols!

[1] Yone Santo, Chap. XXII.

generally would do well to copy. They are useful in showing the natives of this land that domestic life is possible without looseness and irregularity. . . . . They cannot help remarking that the missionary element is disfigured by none of the licentiousness which is their own bane, and against which they take too little pains to guard themselves. The lesson is a sound and wholesome one, and I am not aware that it is taught by any other section of the foreign community. To that extent the missionaries are in a high degree useful. They preach the virtues of morality, and in their practice they offer a model to be respected, if it cannot be followed by the laity."

According to House, then, the service of the missionaries consists solely in purifying the home. He is, in a large degree, correct. This, in truth, has been the greatest secular good which Christianity has conferred upon humanity; and if missionaries can transplant to Asiatic soil the idea of a Christian Home, well do they deserve the name of the servants of the Lord. Already this service has been performed in a small measure, as is manifest in their warm interest in the cause of education, in the elevation of the status of woman, in social reforms, and even in international fair dealing. This we say with no desire to exalt the humanitarian aspect of Christianity above the uplifting power of its spiritual nature; for, after all, the sublimest message conveyed to man is that which convinces him of sin and reveals in Christ "the fulness of the Godhead bodily."

Agriculture.

An old country whose resources are chiefly agricultural, owing to the long-continued policy of self-contentment, Japan has little to learn from outside, especially from America, in the subject of intensive cultivation. But of knowledge of extensive agriculture, the Japanese farmers had little if any. With the exception of horses for military use and cattle as beasts of burden, the breeding of domestic animals was not practical to any great extent. Vast fertile plains suited for grazing were therefore left untouched, if they were not irrigable. Capacity to grow rice was almost the sole criterion of the utility of a given tract of land.[1]

The Island of Hokkaido (Yeso) is not well adapted for raising this staple crop, and, with an area as large as Scotland, its virgin fertility long remained dormant, attracting scarcely any immigration. Its rich coal mines were little worked, its fisheries gave occupation to a small migratory population of Northern Hondo (main Island). Hokkaido was thus economically beyond the Taifoon circle, but as it is so near the Russian frontier, it is not politically prudent to neglect its better colonization. To carry on this work, when a Department of Colonization was created, with General Kuroda at its head, the Commissioner of Agriculture in Washington was secured as adviser.

A son of Dr. Seth Capron, whose name is identified with the establishment of the first woolen factory in the United States, GENERAL HORACE CAPRON is connected with the introduction of the American farming system into Japan. He came in 1873, with a staff of scientific specialists. Their work was first geological, mining, hydrographic and trigonometrical surveys of the Island. New industries were brought into being. Several American crops were raised with success; American breeds of cattle, horses, sheep and hogs were imported. Nowhere in the Empire are American influences more deeply stamped and localized than in the Island of Hokkaido, and this was, in the main, due to General Capron and his staff. Better than the Second Order of the Rising Sun, which was bestowed upon him at the expiration of his service, is the appreciation of General Capron's work as expressed in Minister Bingham's letter[2] to him, and which,

---

[1] For the detailed study of Japanese agricultural systems, see the author's monograph, *Ueber den Japanischen Grundbesitz*, Berlin, 1890.
[2] Dated January, 1875. The writer is indebted to Mrs. Capron for kindly showing him the MSS. autobiography, as well as other papers and documents, of her honored husband.

with some allowance for its eulogistic character, is very true : "Long after you shall have joined[1] those who have gone before you, when Yesso shall be covered with cattle and sheep and fields of golden wheat and corn, and its mountains clothed to their summits with the purple vine, will it be said of you, 'this was the work of General Capron.'"

During his connection with the Colonial Government, General Capron laid the foundation of an agricultural school, which was, in 1876, developed into a college by COLONEL WILLIAM S. CLARK, PH. D., LL. D., then President of the Massachusetts Agricultural College. Dr. Clark was invited, with the assistance of several young men whom he took with him as instructors of the infant college, to organize it after the plan of his institution in Amherst. The College has proved so successful that, in spite of several changes in the administration of the Island, it has continued in vigorous existence.

Messrs. WILLIAM WHEELER, of Concord, D. P. PENHALLOW, now professor in Montreal, WILLIAM P. BROOKS, now of Amherst, Mass., CECIL H. PEABODY, now of the Institute of Technology, Boston, have all rendered valuable service in connection with the College.

Fish-canning, which has become quite an industry in Hokkaido, received much assistance from MR. ULYSSES TREAT, of Maine, while the manufacture of beet-sugar was begun at the instance of Colonel Clark. The American agricultural machines brought by Perry, were, strange to say, first used on the Island of Hokkaido, in 1868, by a German farmer—Mr. Gärtner.

In the Main Island, the experiment of stock breeding, more especially of sheep, was entrusted to an American gentleman, MR. D. W. AP JONES, who, in 1873, imported some fine stock from various countries, to set an example in sheep-raising in the vicinity of Tokyo.

---

[1] General Capron died in Washington, D. C., February, 1886.

MR. RISLEY, known as "Professor" Risley, who came to Japan in 1864 in charge of a circus, having failed in this vocation, became a dairyman two years later and is worthy of being mentioned, as he was the first to pursue that calling in Japan. His dairy and the ice-house soon passed to other hands, while he rushed to the United States and England as a manager of a Japanese acrobatic troupe.

CAPTAIN L. L. JANES was instrumental in introducing agricultural implements and machinery from the United States, into the southern part of Japan, and in encouraging the cultivation of madder.

Of American crops cultivated in Japan, corn and potatoes, though both of them were acclimatised some centuries ago, are important renewed contributions to the agricultural resources of the country. Fruit trees—especially apple, pear and plum; grape-vines and vegetables—such as some kinds of squashes, cabbages and onions; forest trees—the locust, larch and hickory, have all been grown with success. Grasses, especially Kentucky blue grass, timothy and clover, imported from the United States, thrive luxuriantly.

American Railways.

Nothing practical came of the engagement which the Shogunate is said[1] to have made with some American trading diplomatists for the construction of a railway. In the fall of 1876, Mr. William Wheeler, then Professor of Mathematics in the College at Sapporo, made a survey of a route between Sapporo and Otaru. A report[2] thereon was submitted to the local authorities early in the ensuing year, but no practical step was taken.

The first American railway—not only the first American railway in Japan, but also the first in the East—was con-

---

[1] Mossman, *New Japan*, 392.
[2] Published in *First Annual Report of Sapporo Ag'l College*, 1877.

structed under the supervision of COLONEL JOSEPH URY CRAWFORD, engineer of the Pennsylvania R. R. Co. His principal assistants were young Japanese graduates of the Troy Polytechnic Institute. Not only was it supervised by an American, but it was equipped with American rolling stock; the iron rails, however, were bought from England. The engines were from the Baldwin Locomotive Works, Philadelphia. The speedy execution of the work—a line of 45 miles, from the harbor of Otaru to the coal mines of Poronai—was accomplished in about two years (1882). This feature of the enterprise and its small expense, were subjects of much admiration on one hand, and of calumniating remarks on the other. The work, if not elegant, is skilfully done. The gradient was quite steep, and the line has the sharpest curves of any line in the country, exciting no small surprise among the engineers in the Main Island. Its apparent crudeness may be fully excused on account of its extreme cheapness, the actual cost being about $20,000 a mile, including everything, whereas other roads cost from two to five times as much.

After the completion of the work, Mr. Crawford was requested by the government to make a reconnoitering trip through the north-eastern half of Hondo. Besides other works, he also prepared an elaborate report on the water supply of the city of Hakodate.

Miscellaneous Services.

In legal matters, MR. E. PESHINE SMITH was, for some time after 1871, a counsellor on International Law. MR. G. W. HILL, an American lawyer, proved himself useful, especially in connection with the Maria Louisa case.[1] Messrs.

---

[1] Early in August, 1872, the attention of the Japanese government was called by the British Chargé d'Affaires to a Peruvian bark, which put into Yokohama under stress of weather. The ship was engaged in the coolie traffic. Two of the 232 Chinese coolies on board, made an attempt to escape, and swam to the shore. On being informed of the fact, the Japanese gov-

VEEDER, TERRY, MCCARTER and others, filled the chair of jurisprudence in the University. Messrs. DENISON and D. W. STEVENS, American Secretaries in the Japanese Legation at Washington, have exerted themselves in the treaty revision conferences, as well as in other affairs.

In Finance, MR. GEORGE B. WILLIAMS was for some years in the service of the Japanese government, and it was in his company that Mr. Yoshida visited the United States in 1872, to contract loans for the Japanese government. MR. MATTHEW SCOTT was also in the employ of the Finance Department. He died in Kobe in 1880, and his remains were taken to San Francisco. The coinage system, in successful operation[1] since 1871, was based on the model of American currency. The banking laws, as well as the patent regulations, were in principle adopted from America.

In naval matters, the service of GENERAL LE GENDRE, for some time United States Consul in Amoy, and now foreign adviser to the government of Corea, was secured when the Formosan Expedition was taking place in 1874. LIEUT. COMMANDER CASSELL, U. S. N., was offered at this time the rank of Commodore of the Japanese Navy, and LIEUTENANT WASSON, formerly of United States Engineers, was also given a position. An American steamer, *New York*, was chartered for the conveyance of troops; but the charter was subsequently cancelled. These American gentlemen, however, upon the interference of the United States Minister, did not take any actual part in the Formosan campaigns. General Le Gendre continued in the Japanese service for some years after the Expedition, and was once sent to the court of

---

ernment stepped in to prevent the iniquitous transactions of the trade within its territorial jurisdiction. Believing in the righteousness of the step, the Japanese government defied the threatenings of Peru and in the end came out victorious. She won the thanks of China, the approbation of the civilized world and, at last, the good will of Peru herself.

[1] The mint at Osaka, however, was bought from Hong-Kong. It is of English make and was set up by an English expert, Captain Kinder.

China, as a bearer of Japanese greetings to the Emperor of the Middle Kingdom upon the occasion of his marriage.

In journalism, soon after Hyogo was opened, MR. WAINEWRIGHT, a gentleman well known in China and in San Francisco, started the *Hyogo News*. His death occurred when the *Hyogo Maru* was lost in the entrance of the Bay of Yedo (June, 1869). MR. HOUSE, formerly of the editorial staff of the *New York Herald*, has conducted the *Tokyo Times*, to the great credit of the paper. DR. F. W. EASTLAKE began and edited the *Tokyo Independent*, a weekly publication truly independent in its attitude. Dr. Eastlake being himself a philologist, the paper mirrors the fact in its polyglot character— the leaders and correspondences being in Japanese, English and German. There are a few small religious periodicals, in which American missionaries take direct or indirect part.

To an American is also due (most probably) an invention for which many thousand Japanese may be temporarily thankful. The idea of an enlarged perambulator was suggested by one MR. GOBLE,[1] and his thought matured in the so-called "man-power carriage" (jin-riki-sha), first used in 1867 or 1868.

When GENERAL U. S. GRANT, during his tour around the world, came to Japan, he rendered a most valuable service in reconciling Japan and China on the question of suzerainity over the Loochoo Islands, a question which was then distracting the two nations. General Adam Badeau tells us how deeply and favorably Grant was impressed with Japan,[2] and

---

[1] Mr. Goble first came to Japan in Perry's squadron, as a marine. On his return to the States he was educated as a missionary, in which capacity he again went to Japan. He was just such a man as would suggest a jin-riki-sha, being practical, plain and rather rough in his thought and action. Cf. Black, *Young Japan*, Vol. II, 312. A Japanese authority (Mr. Kurokawa) states that the jin-riki-sha was first made in 1871, by two wainwrights in Tokyo.

[2] Speaking of the nation he said: "This is a most beautiful country and a most interesting people. The progress they have made in their changed civilization within 12 years, is almost incredible. . . . This is marvellous,

aside that, could he again have reached the Presidency, it would have been his principal object of administration to inaugurate many and large ideas he then formed concerning the Oriental policy.

Lastly, a few literary influences. Some English words have been added to the Japanese vocabulary. They are mostly monosyllabic, and are words of daily occurrence; hence they are more convenient to use than their translations, as, for instance, pen, ink, knife, fork, hat, cap, stick, milk, butter, etc. In treaty-ports, among the coolie class *Pidjin* (from the Chinese pronunciation of "business") *English* is quite common. The plan of transliteration—spelling Japanese words in Roman characters, and thus disposing of the use of cumbrous Chinese characters and of Japanese syllabification—finds its strong advocates and supporters among Americans; notably, Professor W. D. Whitney, in his letter "on the adoption of English language in Japan."[1]

American Writers on Japan.

In the course of our narrative we have had occasion to become acquainted with MR. KING, of the American house of King & Co., Macao. We have learned, too, of his errand of mercy, how it was planned and how it failed. He published his experience in the *Voyage of the Morrison* in 1837. Throughout the description of his treatment in Japanese waters and his reflections thereon, we notice a vein of kindly Christian spirit.

---

when the treatment these people and all Eastern peoples receive at the hands of the average foreigners residing among them, is considered. I have never been so struck with the heartlessness of nations, as well as individuals, as since coming to the East. But a day of retribution is sure to come."

[1] See *Education in Japan*, pp. 144-153. See also J. Edkins, *The Nature of Japanese Language and its Possible Improvements*, Trans. Asia. Soc. of J., 96, in which he hails with delight the introduction (and eventually, as it seems, the adoption?) of the English language in Japan.

He calls upon his countrymen to direct their religious and commercial efforts to their eastern neighbor. "America," he says, "is the hope of Asia beyond the Malayan peninsula, and her noblest efforts will find a becoming theatre there." There is not much reason, however, to suppose that his passionate appeals were heeded by his compatriots.

Equally unheeded were the meditations on board the *Morrison*, which a companion of King's—the medical missionary DR. PETER PARKER, now of Washington, D. C.—embodied in the *Journal of an Expedition*, London, 1838.

After the appearance of these two works, there was a long dearth of American authorship relative to Japan, until a writer under the nom de plume of PHILOLETHES, brought into the book market his *Justo Ucondono*. Issued by a Catholic publisher in Baltimore, in 1854, it is intended to portray the life of a Christian (Roman Catholic) prince in Japan. Some of its characters are apparently drawn from our history; but, compared with Lady Fullerton's similar attempt (*Laurentia*), it is an exceedingly poor and confused production.

The meagreness of the historical knowledge of "Philolethes" is not at all to be wondered at, when even such a laborious scholar as RICHARD HILDRETH could elucidate our history and geography so little in his *Japan as it was and is*. Hildreth's interest in this far-off land was aroused while "collecting materials for a biography of the first settlers and planters of New England and Virginia," a fact which reminds us how, later, Mr. Vining came to treat of Japan so extensively, in his attempt (*Inglorious Columbus*) to prove that the first discoverer of the American continent came from Asia.

Hildreth was soon followed by BAYARD TAYLOR, who completed the record of his two-and-a-half years' travel, in his *India, China and Japan*, which was published in 1855. He was in Perry's Squadron, somewhat in the capacity of a secretary. "In accordance with the special regulations issued by the Secretary of the Navy," he says, "I was obliged to give up my journals to the Department at the close of my connection with the Expedition." The book named above contains, therefore, chiefly the crumbs that fell from the table; but it shows the keen perception of human and national characteristics which he possessed. Later, in 1881, he edited a serial work, of which *Japan in our Day* is a part.

Another man who took part in the Expedition, J. W. SPALDING, a clerk to the captain of the flag-ship, collected his "crumbs" in such a form and amount as to cater to the humorous propensities of the public. His *Japan Expedition*, 1855, shows in its roguish treatment of his experiences and observations a similarity to a German book by Maron, *China and Japan*.

An artist of the Expedition, WILLIAM HEINE, a German in nationality, but whom we shall here number among American writers on Japan, inasmuch as he was taken in the Squadron, threw a side light on the country by means of his pictures and *Graphic Scenes in the Japan Expedition*, published in 1856. Heine wrote several works on Japan in his mother tongue.

The last-named three American works contained the personal experiences of the individuals whose names they bear, whereas the *Narrative of the Expedition of an American Squadron to the China Seas and Japan* was published by order of Congress, in 1856, as an official account of Perry's mission. The whole work consists of four thick quarto volumes. To avoid any possible partiality in the compilation of such a work, which would likely be the case were it entrusted to anyone who took part in it, a disinterested party—namely, Francis L. Hawks, D. D., LL. D., was chosen, and in his hands were placed all the materials from the pens of Commodore Perry and of his staff. The narrative part, constituting Volume I, gives the minutest details of the Expedition, to satisfy, as the compiler says, "the natural curiosity of his countrymen to know every particular of the story." Volume II contains the Natural History of Japan, while Volume III deals with astronomical observations, and Volume IV with hydrographical matters. Interesting as this ponderous work is to interested parties, its bulk forbade its popularity and hence Dr. Hawks' assistant,

ROBERT TOMES, M. D., abridged the account in his *Americans in Japan* (1860).

The literary activity immediately following the Perry Expedition did not end with Dr. Tomes. The fame which attended this event, called forth from the hand of AARON H. PALMER a little pamphlet on the *Origin of the Mission to Japan* (1859), in which he set forth his own claims to recognition as a principal agent in its preparation.

From the beginning of 1860, American literature on Japanese subjects dates—only to wane again for nearly a decade. The only works which belong to this period, are CHARLES C. COFFIN's juvenile book *Our New Way round the World*, and RAPHAEL PUMPELLY's *Across America and Asia* (5th ed., 1871). In the former, its author describes the Japan of 1868, through which he and his wife passed. In the latter, eight long chapters are devoted to Japan, with an additional one on art prepared by JOHN LA FARGE, who, by the way, at present contributes a series of *Artist's Letters from Japan* to the *Century Magazine*. An able scientist and close observer, and for some years a resident in the country, Professor Pumpelly treats the land and people of Japan with fairness and candor. Though many things that he noted in his book, have since passed away, it is still suggestive because of this spirit and method of treatment.

During the decade 1870–80, American pens were busily engaged in matters concerning Japan. Indeed it might be exalted to an epoch, since Griffis' work then appeared.

We begin the writers of the seventies with the illustrious name of WILLIAM H. SEWARD, whose *Travels around the World* (1873), edited by his adopted daughter, Olive Risley Seward, contain interesting accounts of Japan, especially of the court as it was in those years of rapid transition. Giving the impressions of a sharp and sagacious statesman, the book still possesses a value which such works as *Life and Adventures in Japan* (1875), by E. WARREN CLARK, or *Grandma's Letters from Japan* (1877), by MRS. MARY PRUYN, have not. Mr. Clark was a teacher from 1871 to '75 in a government school, and Mrs. Pruyn a missionary during the same period. In their respective capacities they could naturally see but little, and consequently their writings are only of passing interest. The same remark applies to the *Sun-Rise Kingdom* (1879), by MRS. J. D. CARROTHERS, in which this missionary lady describes woman's work for woman in Japan.

In 1877, appeared *From Egypt to Japan*, by H. M. FIELD, D. D., in which this experienced traveller divine touches upon the recent changes in Japan.

By far the best American work on Japan, not only in the decade we have just been considering, but also in the whole range of American (and in some sense of Western) authorship on the subject, is the *Mikado's Empire*, by WM. ELLIOT GRIFFIS, D. D., now a Congregational minister in Boston. Griffis was elected by the Faculty of Rutgers College to proceed to Japan as a teacher in the daimiate of Echizen, when application was made therefrom in 1868. He accepted the post, and soon found himself in the midst of ardent and fruitful labors. On his return to America he brought forth the *Mikado's Empire*, as a result of his four years of close study. He does not himself deny the great help he received from his Japanese friends, and this very fact makes his statements the more trustworthy. Griffis does not claim any originality of historical research or scientific investigation, in which respects he is surpassed by a few later and foreign writers. No author has done more to present in attractive style the salient features of our tradition, history, manners and customs. Sir Edward Reed attempted a task similar to his, in *Japan, its History, Traditions and Religions* (2 vols., London, 1880), with much success, but not approaching that of Griffis. The latter has passed through several editions (5th ed., 1886), and its worn-out condition in many a public library, attests how diligently and deservedly it is perused. By means of the appendices, Dr. Griffis keeps up with the rapidly progressing changes of the country. The many articles he contributes to leading periodicals of the Union, his more recent works on *Corea, the Hermit Nation*, and the *Life of Commodore M. C. Perry* (revised edition, 1890), are the indirect outcome of his studies of and in Japan.

If Griffis has rendered valuable service in enlightening the reading public of his country regarding the Mikado's Empire, EDWARD GREEY has taken upon himself the task of teaching to the "young folks," the interesting features in the life of their neighbor nation. An Englishman by birth, but naturalized a citizen of New York, where he was well known as an art dilettante and an author of popular plays, he is a successful interpreter of Japan to the juvenile readers of his adopted country. So earnestly was he bent upon this mission, that he gave his infant daughter a Japanese name. Though he was only a short time in the *Wonderful City of Tokio*, he describes it well, and in such a way as to entertain children by its oddities. He pursues the same object in his *Young Americans in Japan, Bear Worshippers of Yeso, Lotus Flowers and Other Stories*. Greey translated, too, the *Loyal Ronins*, a tale of Feudal Japan, and *the Captive of Love*, a work of Bakin.

Almost as entertaining to children as Greey's books in its many illustrations and easy diction, but of totally different object and character of contents, is a work of the HON. JOHN RUSSEL YOUNG, ex-minister to China. He was companion to General Grant in his travels, and, in his book bearing the title *Around the World with General Grant* (2 vols.), he devotes several chapters to Japan. Containing, as it does, the keen observations of Mr. Young himself and the ripe judgment of Mr. Grant, the work is of more special interest than an ordinary work of travel. Even as a private citizen of the Union, Grant's words bore almost official weight. His enthusiastic reception by the high and the low in Japan, his repeated and confidential interviews with the Emperor and Ministers of State, his good offices in matters relating to China and Japan, his assurance of American interest in and sympathy for the East, rendered his character both popular and respected, and the account of his travels almost documentary in importance.

A colleague of Mr. Grant, GENERAL CHARLES W. LE GENDRE, who, as has been said, was several years in the employ of the Japanese government, expressed his solicitude for the future of Japan in his *Progressive Japan; a Study of Political and Social Needs of the Empire* (1878). The main object of the work is to warn the Japanese against radical changes—not to mistake a form for a principle of liberal government. The part treating of the improvement of agriculture, is a careful study of the financial condition of the time in which he wrote, and bears the character of an economic monograph on agriculture, whereas

THOMAS B. VAN BUREN's *Labor and Porcelain in Japan* (1882) is a very good study of manufactures, which he, in the capacity of Consul General, could investigate in detail. Let it be stated, in passing, that in the *Consular Reports, Foreign Relations* and other government publications, is found much invaluable information upon all subjects relating to Japanese industries and commerce.

One versatile and highly gifted writer on Japan is next to be mentioned. MR. EDWARD H. HOUSE, a New York journalist of no mean reputation, had long been interested in Japan, and "to seek his love in the far East"—to quote the words of the Hon. John R. Young[1]—"he had left a career of promise and renown. House has given himself to Japan with a spirit that I might call the missionary spirit of self-abnegation. He has fought her battles. . . . . He has accepted contumely and misrepresentation in her cause, for I found—

---

[1] *Around the World with General Grant*, Vol. II, p. 591.

how quickly you find it out!—that if you take sides with the Eastern nations in this far East, you bring upon you the rancor of foreigners." How true his estimate of House is, we easily find in the writings of the latter. By far the best articles from the pen of House are his two papers in the *Atlantic Monthly*, the *Martyrdom of an Empire* (May, 1881) and the *Thraldom of Japan* (December, 1887), both of which are clear, concise presentations of the financial and political strait into which the unjust treaties of foreign powers have brought our nation. He contributed articles of similar import to the *New Princeton Review*. All these are instructive in the highest degree, in showing the dealings of Western, so-called Christian powers with eastern "heathen" peoples. But House is not always grave; in his *Japanese Episodes*, he entertains his readers with incidents of his sojourn in Japan, where, beside his editorial career, he spent some time as a professor in the University. In his latest story, *Yone Santo; a Child of Japan*, he assumes not only the above mentioned tasks of enlightening the Christian public as to the fundamental error in the family system of Japan, and the inadequacy of those American teachers of the Gospel who undertake to reform it, but also gives us, through the words which he puts into the mouth of his heroine, a glimpse of the moral traits which feudalism developed in the Japanese character.

MR. LOUIS WERTHEIMBER, who was several years in the employ of our government, and is at present a dealer in antiques in New York, has had in view a similar object of interpreting feudal influences, in his *Muramasa Blade*.

Again, the character engendered by Feudalism, and yet modified by the new era, is illustrated in short sketches by CHARLES LANMAN, in his *Leading Men of Japan*. As American Secretary to the Japanese Legation in Washington, for the eleven years including and subsequent to 1871, Mr. Lanman had, in this capacity, access to Japanese documents and acquaintance with the diplomatic corps, and was thus in a position to give the world brief chapters in the biographies of some forty of our public men. His first systematic literary work in his capacity as Secretary to the Legation, was the preparation of a volume on the *Resources of America*, which was published in Mori's name for circulation in Japan. Then appeared *The Japanese in America*, giving an account of the Iwakura Embassy, of the Hon. Arinori Mori, and of some young students of both sexes.

Etchings from Two Lands (1886) is a work by MRS. CLARA MASON, who describes her experience of a sojourn in Japan, whither she went with her husband in 1873 as a missionary.

The year 1886 brought before the public another volume on Japan. ARTHUR C. MACLAY, a young lawyer in New York, for some years (1873-8) a teacher in Japan, recounts in his *Budget of Letters from Japan* (2d ed., 1890) what he saw, heard and felt. In an easy, genial tone, he conveys quite interesting information. Mr. Maclay is also the author of another work—*The Mito Yashiki*, in which he contrasts "the old pagan Japan" with the new "Christian" Japan, taking the conservative capitol of Mito for the scene of his story.

Quite unique in its character is the work of PROFESSOR EDWARD S. MORSE—*Japanese Homes and their Surroundings*. One of the best scientists of America, he has opened by this book a new field of studies and an untried chapter in Sociology. It is not too much to say with the *American Architect*, that " the author has brought to the task a spirit of catholic sympathy, an indefatigable patience of investigation, a clear head, a mind full of frankness and good humor, and, not least, the hand of an accomplished artist in graphic delineation." Professor Morse has written a large number of articles on Japan. Those on scientific themes appeared mostly in *Popular Science Monthly* and *Nature*; those on social or political subjects have come out in various New England newspapers. He has now in preparation a work on Japanese porcelain.

The latest American writer of any importance is PERCIVAL LOWELL, author of the *Soul of the Far East* (1888) and *Chosön* (1886). In the former he pretends to have gauged, after a few months' study, the genius of the people and of the institutions of Eastern Asia. In a dashy, quasi-philosophical series of essays, he attempts to prove that the soul of the far East is impersonal. His statements, sweeping and shallow as they are, are accompanied here and there by a few bright thoughts, and are conveyed in beautiful language.

Mr. Percival Lowell is not, however, the only superficial writer on Japan. Too many persons hastily jot down the impressions of their brief sojourn, during which their ignorance of the native tongue keeps them from coming into close contact with the people; generalize on their scanty observations, and, on their return home, publish them without much discretion. Hence the so-called "facts" or "impressions" and "experiences," as well as woodcuts and other illustrations, are too apt to convey erroneous ideas and mislead the reading public.

On the whole, it must be candidly confessed that American works on Japan, with a few exceptions, have not done much credit to American scholarship. As Professor Nichol says of American literature in general, so it is that American works on our country are intended for general reading and not for study. Many of them are mere narratives and autobiographical chapters of ordinary persons, who studied Japanese life much as "a frog does the sky from within a well." Works which can bear the strict test of scientific criticism, are very rare, and it is in this respect that the writings of Englishmen like Anderson, Satow and Chamberlain, or of Germans like Rein, Liebscher and Siebold, are superior to anything that American authors have undertaken.

There are, however, some pleasant features in the writings of American authors on our country. One feature is freedom from national prejudices against Japan and from undue national braggadocio and Chauvinism; hence Americans are generally more sympathetic and just than others, in their appreciation and delineation of Japanese character. Another distinguishing peculiarity is the strong admixture of religious interests which they evince—a feature due to the fact that the authors are chiefly missionaries or teachers.

American bibliography on Japan is thus calculated to cement the friendly feelings already existing between the two nations. Its mission is not a philosophical or historical research—but a genial and humane bond; it is not intellectual—but moral, not science—but love.

Dark Side of Foreign Influence.

As the vessels of Perry's Squadron steamed out of the harbor of Shimoda, after their mission had been fulfilled, Dr. Williams jotted down in his note-book: "God grant that in opening their country to the West, we may not be bringing upon them misery and ruin!"[1] Four years later, Lord Elgin, who was on a similar errand, is said to have exclaimed the same in the same harbor. The fears of Williams and Elgin were, and are still, shared by many—and justly so, because the contact of two peoples of different grades or kinds of civilisation, has so often been fraught with most deplorable consequences to the weaker party. The greater the difference between the two parties, the more disastrous has the contact often proved to the feebler. Williams and Elgin, being unaccustomed to the quaint forms of our civilisation, might have looked upon them as manifestations of barbarism; hence their solicitude about "misery" and "ruin" to our nation, was likely magnified.

The truth is, however, that notwithstanding the hue and cry raised by the Jô-i (exclusion) faction—and lately revived by the Koku-zui-Hoson (Nationalist) party—the dark side of foreign intercourse fades before the light from its brighter side. Alarmists and pessimists resort to exaggeration, and the small dark spots assume in their eyes appalling dimensions.

---

[1] *Life and Letters*, 223.

It is not, however, Alarmists and Chauvinists alone that detect much to complain of, in the influences of Western culture upon their nation. Cool-headed men, both at home and abroad, have given expression to the same solicitude. Only lately has Lord Eustace Cecil said: "The danger is that all the luxuries, vices and discontent of European life may be also introduced. Heaven forbid that this should be so, or that the frugal modes of living, patriarchal politeness, and respect for authority of this most interesting and marvelous people, should disappear under the withering influence of European (and we might add American) contact."[1]

The precipitous and indiscriminate way in which Western culture was adopted—and not the culture itself—is greatly to blame. It is the old story of the new wine put into old wine-skins.

Into the old, time-worn wine-skin of feudal bondage, isolated repose and military lethargy, was suddenly poured the new wine of individual liberty, international commerce and industrial activity; who can wonder if the wine-skin bursts? We will briefly glance at its rents.

Feudalism, if it failed as a political system, has nevertheless, as a social one, ever developed many and noble moral qualities.[2] Unlike the present individualistic organization of society, where the daily relation of man with man is debited and credited with cash, feudalism bound men by personal ties to their fellows; hence personal loyalty, strong sense of honor, proud contempt of money, chivalrous admiration of valor and stoicism, military decision of character and heroic abnegation of self, were some of the traits which Feudalism nurtured. These, of course, have their undesirable extremes, but even these extremes are preferable to those of their counter qualities.

---

[1] *The Nineteenth Century*, Dec., 1888, p. 862.
[2] See an eloquent defence of Feudalism by Adam Müller, who speaks of it as an essentially Christian institution. *Elemente der Staatskunst*, Berlin, 1809, Pt. II, 72–99.

Now, when the doctrine that "all men are born free and equal"—a phraseology susceptible of grossest misconstruction—creeps in, acknowledgment of superiority, personal loyalty, that virtue of reverence without which, as Carlyle has well said, no society can exist, are likely to vanish. Fortunately, however, owing to the temperate disposition of our people, the influences of American ideas of liberty and equality were never so disastrous as in the country of Madame Roland. Nevertheless, they have had in a small way their distorted fruits among the youths. "O Liberty! how many crimes are committed in thy name!"

By far the most noticeable moral effect of the opening of foreign intercourse, has been the rapid disappearance of native politeness, without its loss being supplied by western ideas of etiquette. This has been the resultant of several forces. Some unappreciative foreigners ridicule many a Japanese act of courtesy; many a native discards it, because he thinks, as does Mr. Spencer, that ceremonial institutions (and politeness is confused with them) are outcroppings of primitive barbarism; others begin the adoption of western customs by unlearning the first requisite of Japanese social life. Equality versus manners!

Closely allied to the ideas of Liberty and Equality, is the principle of Individualism, which Percival Lowell claims as a moral monopoly of the Western races. Noble quality as it is, it too has its dark side, especially noticeable to a society in the weaving of whose tissues duty was the warp and personal devotion the woof. At its touch, even family ties disintegrate; no wonder then, that in Mr. Lowell's country it is not a rare occurrence for brother to enter law-suit against brother, for a paltry pittance of inheritance!

Concomitant with Individualism is modern Industrialism, towards which, according to Mr. Herbert Spencer, all society advances. This, as is best typified by America, necessarily elevates the estimate and the esteem of money, while the exaltation of commerce likewise contributes to this end. The absence of the love of money has been a great drawback to the economic development of our people; but its extreme, Mammonism, is to be as carefully avoided as, within rational limits, an appreciation of its importance is to be encouraged. Too much is now-a-days preached about the value of money;—as though man and the State can live by bread alone.

To be sure, America has given us more than the material elements of civilization. She has taught us Religion, and to the dark side of religious influences allusion has already been made. She has taught us, too, both Science and Philosophy, though here again the evil which accompanies them lies in materialism and agnosticism. For this, however, English and German thought is more responsible. The moral influences of the West have likewise been negative, or at best utilitarian. In other words, the unfruitful "profit-and-loss philosophy" of logic-choppers has displaced the more natural and beautiful teachings of the ancient sages of the East; it has been adopted by many votaries in preference to the simple, yet sublime precepts, which it has been the endeavor and prayer of the purest minds of the West to teach the East.

Respecting the introduction of western usages, manners and customs, it may be worth while to say a word and that by no means an encouraging one. Much has lately been said in foreign papers about change of female costume in Japan. It cannot be denied that it needs reform, and those kindly-meaning American ladies who discouraged it, simply because Japanese dress is "quaint," "pretty," "picturesque," etc., forget that dress has a more utilitarian object than to please the eye. At the same time, it was sheer folly on the part of Japanese reformers (?) to adopt the very absurdities of Western women, which the more sensible among them reject—corsets and superfluities, to wit. Moreover, the poorer Japanese can ill afford to keep up with the fashions of their richer trans-Pacific sisters. Since improvements in the present costume are needed, why not go to our own forefathers; or, if there is fascination in borrowing, why not borrow of ancient Greece or of neighboring China?

As to male costume, it is somewhat different. Our flowing garb, with its long sleeves and loose gowns, is extremely hindering to active movement, and is not, therefore, adapted to practical purposes. The Western suit, on the contrary, is designed for use, although it is far from being artistic or graceful. The adoption of coat and pantaloons, then, by the Japanese, is decidedly an advantage in their every-day work; but to have made "swallow-tails" and "stove-pipes" a requisite of ceremonial attire—that is a burlesque in its most ridiculous form.

Equally ludicrous is Western dancing, in the manner and extent of its adoption by us. How much comelier are our own classical dances, compared with the acrobatic hoppings of dizzy men and women in the crowded salon of a ball! To justify such performances on the ground of health, is a poor excuse indeed.

As to masquerades, frequently given in the highest circle of our society, no excuse is possible, even though they are imported directly from the royal courts of the West. They are a violence to human dignity and nothing short of an abomination.

Guard as we may against importing the tares, these come with the wheat, and the soil gives ample nourishment to both. The growth of the tares among us, is often a subject of ridicule and sarcasm by foreign journalists and writers, who freely indulge in the use of such words as "apish," "imitative," "morbidly denationalizing," "delirious," and others of a similar or more vehement import, as though there were in the very constitution of the Japanese character a defect. Let these learn of history, and ponder over the French influences in England after the restoration of Charles II, the French influences in Prussia at the time of no less a ruler than

Frederick the Great,—or over the State of Italy during the Renaissance, or over the foreign influences in Russia under Peter the Great. If the tares throve luxuriantly on these fields, it only showed the fertility of the soil. Meanwhile, let Young Japan remember that national life is ever continuous, that the heritage of the *Spirit of Yamato* is hers, and that this spirit, consecrated to divine purpose, should be the earnest of her future.

CHAPTER V.

JAPANESE IN AMERICA.

Before Perry's Expedition.

It is foreign to the object of the present treatise, to attempt any contribution to the many conjectures and theories advanced respecting the immigration of the Japanese race to the American continent. The subject has been discussed by many writers of note; but it is neither exhausted nor settled. Equally out of place in this study, is any detailed narrative of many a shipwrecked sailor or fisherman who was drifted all the way across the Pacific Ocean; but it has been necessary incidentally to make occasional allusions to these, and a few more cases might be cited.

One *Nakahama*,[1] a fisherman, was blown to sea with two companions and wafted to the American coast, about 1841. He remained in the States for ten years, and returned shortly before the arrival of Perry. His acquisition of English procured him an important position as interpreter, which he filled for a short time. He is still living. *Sentaro*—better known by his American nickname, *Sam Patch*—was one of seventeen unfortunates, who, while manning a junk, were blown to sea, rescued by an American vessel and taken to San Francisco. Sam Patch accompanied the Perry Squadron. All the while they sailed, he was apprehending that some ill would befall his neck and was constantly repeating *Shimpai! Shimpai!*

---

[1] For more particulars see Griffis, *Perry*, pp. 361, 366.

(Japanese word for "troubled in mind"), showing with what fear and trembling he came once more to take a glance at his native land. He was asked by the Japanese officials to stay in the country and engage in building "black ships;" but nothing could free him of his *shimpai*, which became almost a part of his constitution, inasmuch as it gave him the sobriquet of *Sam Patch*. He was placed under the care of Mr. J. Goble, who took him to Hamilton, N. Y., where the poor heathen was dubbed a Christian by being dipped into water. In 1860, when Goble came to Japan as a missionary, he took Sam with him; but at that time, when a scrappy knowledge of English might be turned to very good account, Sam lacked Yankee pluck, and he lived and died a poor house-servant. *Dan Ketch* (Japanese name said to be *Dans Kevitch*), or, more properly, *Dan Kichi*, was for some time a companion of Sam. After staying some years in China and America, he returned home, served as an interpreter in the British Legation, and in 1860, as we have seen in the course of our narration, he fell a victim to a *ronin's* sword. Joseph Heco (?) was one of those picked up at sea by an American bark, the Auckland, in 1851. He lived in San Francisco, where he learned the language and some business. He was brought to Washington and to the Atlantic cities for some weeks, and, in 1859, left the States for Japan, where, as a naturalized American, he became a merchant in Yokohama. These are a few of several shipwrecked Japanese in America, whose annals are too short and simple, and in most cases too obscure to be recorded here.[1]

At the time when Perry was in Japan, two young men repaired under covert of night to his ships, and requested him

---

[1] Strange information was furnished the writer by the Rev. Wightman, D. D., of Baltimore, about an oriental who was a member of his church in Columbia, S. C. Dr. Wightman assures the writer that the man, *Adair* or *Adire* by name, was a Japanese gardener by trade, a devout man who prayed while in his country, that he might be taken to a land where he could worship a true God. Shortly after he had made this prayer, Perry's Squadron arrived. Adire requested him to take him to a godly country.

to take them to the States. One of them was no other than
Torajiro Yoshida, a man of great force of character and of
penetrating intellect. Convinced of the superiority of Western civilization, he was eager to see with his own eyes wherein
that superiority consisted. The inclusion law was then in full
force, and it was at the risk of their lives that he and his
comrade dared to be taken on board. Perry refused; much
as he admired their zeal and bravery, he could not shelter
those who violated the law of the land to which he avowed
friendship. Yoshida and his comrade were arrested for the
offence, and shortly after died, greatly lamented and respected.[1]

Shogun's Embassy.

Of more than one embassy sent abroad by the Shogunate,
the one undertaken by the advice of Townsend Harris, and
which left Japan in the spring of 1860 (Feb. 13), was the
most formal. This consisted of Shimmi, the Chief Ambassador, of a Vice-Ambassador, a censor, five minor officials, three
interpreters (among whom was the far-famed "Tommy"),
three physicians and fifty-two attendants—including barbers,
pike-bearers, &c., making a total of seventy-one persons.
After touching at Hawaii for a supply of coal, the Powhatan,
whose service was secured for the conveyance of the Embassy,
sailed from Honolulu and reached the Golden Gate on the
29th of March. During a week's stay in San Francisco, the
hospitalities as well as the curiosity of the American people,
were bestowed upon them. The members of the Embassy,

The Rev. Wm. Martin, of Columbia, writes: "O. Adair came to Columbia, in 1861 or 1862, and was employed as a gardener or florist at the Lunatic Asylum. . . . . I married him to Miss Elizabeth Stuart, daughter of one of the keepers, a pious member of the Methodist church. He attended the service in the chapel, and, in 1868, professed conversion to Christianity and after careful examination I received him into the M. E. Church South, and baptized him. He proved faithful until he died."

[1] For their visit to Perry's Squadron, see Hawks, Perry Expedition.

on their part, evinced their gratification by purchasing carloads of cloths, blankets, carpets, &c. These were taken home by the *Kan-rin-maru*,[1] a small Japanese steamer, which had been dispatched to San Francisco some time before, for the express purpose of ascertaining the safe arrival of the Embassy. As this was the first steamer to cross the Pacific, manned and managed by the Japanese (under the control of Awa Katsu, a present Privy Councillor), the event is not without importance.[2] From San Francisco to Panama, thence across the Isthmus to the Atlantic waters, ran the Embassy's route. Arriving at Hampton Roads, they were transported to Washington *via* the Potomac River, reaching the capital in the middle of May. Here they were most liberally accomodated at Willard's Hotel, every precaution being taken to make their first visit to America comfortable and pleasant. Two days later, they were received by President Buchanan in state. It is needless to repeat the ceremonies and the indispensable speeches of the occasion, or to describe public and private dinners given in their honor, or to follow them as they were taken to places of interest. The local newspapers of the time teem with accounts of them.

---

[1] The graves of two sailors, Tomi-Jow (Tomizo) and Me-Nay-Kee-Tschee (Minekichi), of the Kan-rin-maru, have lately been discovered in the Central Avenue burial-ground in San Francisco.
[2] Mr. Kimura, who served as Chief of the Admiralty under the Shogunate, and who visited the U. S. by this steamer, jots down in his diary: "Hospitality and modesty seem to me to be the distinguishing characteristics of this people (Americans). Even the humblest appear to rejoice that their country has formed a friendly pact with distant Japan" (*Tokyo Independent*, Dec. 25, 1886). He writes to the author,—"Nothing struck me with so much surprise as the genial disposition of the people. Knowing as I did how our government treated foreigners, I expected a reciprocal treatment from the Americans; but what was my surprise when I found them so genial and kind, shaking hands friendlily wherever I went and the children bringing me bouquets. As oft as I thought of the contrast of our treatment of Americans and theirs of us, I blushed and felt ashamed."

In the middle of June, they had a final interview with the President. In commemoration of the visit, medals were struck—of which three in gold were presented to the ambassadors, twenty in silver to the officials of the suite, while the attendants were also honored with bronze ones.

On their way north, they stopped in Baltimore for a day and a night. Here, also, a liberal reception awaited them.[1] In the day-time, they were entertained in the Maryland Institute, and in the evening, from the galleries in Gilmor's (now Guy's) Hotel, their eyes feasted upon the display of fire-works in the Union Square. Their delight, however, cost one of them too dear. A sword of some value was purloined, while they were all absent from the room. At a time when the sword was called "the soul of the samurai," the exasperation of its loser might well be imagined. It was found a year later and returned with an apology from Secretary Seward.

From Baltimore, they proceeded to Philadelphia, exciting all the way no ordinary degree of curiosity. "Tommy" contributed no mean quota to American enthusiasm, by riding on the locomotive and hailing, in a unique manner of his own, the throng along the route, occasionally ringing the bell to give variety to the scene. Their arrival in Philadelphia is thus described by its historians:[2] "On the 9th of June, there was an immense mass of humanity at the Broad and Prime streets Depot, to catch a glimpse of the ambassadors. . . . It was estimated that with the numerous visitors who came to the city from the country, the multitude numbered half a million people. . . . The hospitality of the citizens was practically unbounded; indeed during that week, there prevailed a 'Japanese fever.' So strong was it that five days after their arrival, councils could not get a quorum together."

Bidding farewell to the Quaker City, they proceeded to the Empire City. Here again, they were received with all that

---

[1] Cost of reception to the City Treasury was $6,164.76 out of $8,000 appropriated for the occasion. *Baltimore Sun*, June 14, 1860.
[2] *Scharf* and *Westcott*, History of Philadelphia, Vol. I, 734.

kindness of heart and freak of fancy could devise to honor and salute them. After a few days of exciting experiences, the Embassy took final leave of the Republic, and we soon see them in the steam-frigate *Niagara* homeward bound.

The avowed object of the mission was the exchange of the ratified treaty of commerce, or, as Griffis says, to obtain a fresh transcript of the Perry treaty, which was burned in the fire of 1858. We doubt from the character of the persons selected for the purpose, that there was any other motive on the part of the Shogunate. But the mere exchange was not the only thing effected in the mission. Among the first lessons that America gave to the minister on his landing at San Francisco, was the high value of Japanese gold coins (which is equivalent to saying the exceedingly low value attached to them at home). He warned his colleagues in Yedo of its efflux. He was struck at the high price of articles of general consumption, and at the wages of American labor, he was amazed. Of the cordiality of American reception, he writes home feelingly. In conclusion, he says on his way to Washington, "though I have not yet seen the Capital, I have already amassed knowledge and experience enough to pile up a mountain or to fill up a sea. But of these, were I to speak with you, three-fourths will be a relation of what I grieve for, for our country." Whatever knowledge or experience Shimmi or his suite might have acquired, they were not the men to put it to practical account, neither was theirs the time. When they returned, the very existence of the Shogunate was at stake, and when it was crushed, they were scattered to the wind.

Imperial Embassy.[1]

"The travelled mind is the catholic mind educated from exclusiveness and egotism." In these words of Alcott, lies a motive which prompted the so-called Iwakura Embassy of 1872. The professed and the wished-for object, however, was

---

[1] A detailed account is given in Lanman's *Japanese in America*.

the revision of the Treaty. In the middle of January, the steamer America arrived at San Francisco with the ambassadorial suite on board. It consisted of forty-nine members, selected from among the most promising of the young statesmen. The lamented Prince Iwakura headed the list, followed by Kido, Okubo and Ito; of these, the first two are no longer living, and the last is now President of the Privy Council. Among others were Mr. Fukuchi, of the *Nichi-Nichi* (*Daily News*), and Mr. Watanabe, late Chancellor of the Imperial University. Commissioners from each department of government also joined them. The Embassy was accompanied by the Hon. Charles E. De Long, then U. S. Minister, and W. S. Rice, Esq., Interpreter in the United States Legation in Japan. From San Francisco, they were accompanied by Mr. Charles W. Brooks, who had for many years served the Japanese government in the capacity of a Commercial Agent and Consul. In San Francisco and Sacramento, the suite was entertained most cordially. Passing through Chicago, they presented the Mayor with the sum of five thousand dollars, for the benefit of those who were suffering from the late conflagration.

The Embassy reached Washington on the last day of February. Here every preparation for their reception had been made by the United States government, as well as by the Japanese envoy, the Hon. Mori. Congress had appropriated $50,000 for their entertainment, and Mr. Mori had, at the request of the Committees on Foreign Affairs and Appropriations, acquainted the two Houses with the particulars of the late movements in his country; of course intimating that his compatriots looked upon the United States as occupying the highest rank among the Treaty Powers.

Early next month, the Embassy had an audience with President Grant, when its credentials were presented, and mutual assurances of friendship and good-will were exchanged. On the sixth, a formal reception was given in the Hall of the House of Representatives. Mr. James G. Blaine, as

Speaker, congratulated the guests on their safe arrival. "The course of migration for the human race," so said he in his address, "has for many centuries been steadily westward, a course always marked by conquest, and too often by rapine. Reaching the boundary of our continent, we encountered a returning tide from your country setting eastward, seeking not the trophies of war, but the more shining victories of peace; and these two currents of population appropriately meet and mingle on the shores of the great Pacific sea."

Under the official escort of the Federal Government, the Embassy, everywhere welcomed, spent the remainder of its stay in America in visiting the cities on the Atlantic coast, and in observing the manners, customs and institutions of the Republic. Its members embarked for Europe, journeying "toward the sunrising, and beholding a new sunrise beyond the one they before enjoyed," as was expressed by one of them.

What did this visit amount to? What has it done? True, it failed in its avowed object. But, on one hand, the Embassy had shown to the world in its brilliant personnel, that Japan was far from being an uncultured nation, while, on the other hand, it returned home (September, 1873) laden with experience and knowledge. Whatever practical schemes of internal improvements or of foreign policy Iwakura, Okubo and others might have planned as the result of their observations abroad, they were prevented from immediate execution of them on account of the question of Korean Invasion, mooted by General Saigo and his party. But that they observed closely in their travel, is evident from the elaborateness of the reports submitted to the government. Consisting of several volumes, these reports have given to the public, then comparatively ignorant of the West, a new and exact idea of America and Europe. The first volume is devoted entirely to the United States. If one may judge from it, the political institutions of the Republic were not what they cared much to learn. A man of the court, "the centralizing Bismarck of

Japan," [1] Prince Iwakura saw in the American constitution only what he would. Nothing, therefore, impressed him more in America than the strength of the central government in Washington, of which Secretary Seward had once made a well-known boast. The reflections in the report are mostly on the social side of American life. The genial disposition of the people in friendly intercourse, their "cosmopolitan character," their practical good sense, the influence which the Protestant religion exerts in society, the system of elementary education, astounding growth of cities, respect paid to women, the immigration of European labor, are all dwelt upon to a greater or less extent.

Influx of Students.

Dr. John M. Ferris,[2] Honorary Secretary of the Board of Foreign Missions of the Reformed Church in America, gives an interesting personal account of how the pioneer Japanese students came to the States, in the autumn of 1866. They (Isé and Numagawa) came to New York with a letter from Dr. G. F. Verbeck. Their intention in coming to America, was "to learn how to build 'big ships' and make 'big guns,' to prevent European powers from taking possession of their country." Even Peter the Great might have blushed to hear that they wanted to carry out this ambitious intention without knowing the language, and, what is worse, with only about one hundred dollars in their pockets. The Board of Foreign Missions, however, took the case in hand; and it was soon resolved that advances should be made from the treasury for their support, and that a house should be found for them in New Brunswick. The young men had

---

[1] For some estimate of Prince Iwakura's character, see an esteemed address by Dr. W. E. Griffis, *Rutgers Graduates in Japan*, p. 13.

[2] See for details Dr. W. E. Griffis, *Rutgers Graduates in Japan*, p. 39, of which I have freely availed myself. For concise account of the Japanese students in U. S., see *Appleton's Annual Cyclopædia*, 1886. Art. Japan.

forfeited their lives by leaving their country without the permission of the authorities, which it was then well-nigh impossible to obtain. When, however, the policy of the government changed, it appropriated money to repay the advances made for them, as well as to continue their studies in comfort. For the following ten years, about five hundred students sought advice or assistance of one kind or another, at the office of the Board of Foreign Missions of the Reformed Church. When the War of the Restoration began, and when some of the students were cut short of their funds, several persons contributed to their support through the Board. These advances were all repaid after the War was ended. Messrs. Iwakura and Okubo, during their ambassadorial tour, made an official acknowledgment to the Board of their kind assistance and generous conduct, " which will do more to cement the friendly relations of the two countries than all other influences combined."

From the circumstances mentioned above, Rutgers College was the first to become the favorite resort of the Japanese; the number who studied there amounting to more than three hundred.

The Naval Academy at Annapolis gave instruction to a few students, who were admitted under special conditions. The De Pauw University, Greencastle, Ind., has been headquarters for such of the Japanese as were sent or supported by Methodist missions. Cornell has some ten Japanese students, most of whom are studying law.

In Ann Arbor, in the grammar and high schools and in the University, there have studied, since 1872, more than forty young men. In the last, the Law Department has been most attended.

Harvard has been sought by some of the brightest youths. From 1871 to the close of 1886, there studied within its halls seven law students, two in the College proper, one in the Medical School, four in the summer course and one B. S. under Professor Gray. The Boston University had also a few Japanese students in the Law and Theological Departments.

In Yale have studied some twenty young men, the principal course taken by them being Law. One young graduate was appointed, in 1867, lecturer in philosophy. Columbia graduated three Ph. Ds. in 1879.

Philadelphia has been a favorite city among the Japanese in the United States. Several attended the late Professor Hastings' School. Here, also, engaged by several railroad companies, notably the Pa. R. R. Co., young engineers have gained practical lessons, which, if not new from their previous training, have added polish to it. The Baldwin Locomotive Works, the Iron Bridge Works in Edge Moor, Delaware, the State Geographical Survey, have also prepared practical workers. The Medical Colleges of the city—the University and the Woman's College—have had Japanese students. The Wharton School of Political Science and Finance, is yearly visited by eager students. The Department of Science of the University graduated an M. E. in 1877.

In Amherst, both the College and the Agricultural College are resorted to by our countrymen. Students of Agriculture are also to be found scattered in different parts of the Union.

Notwithstanding its recent foundation, the Johns Hopkins University has by far the best reputation in Japan. Its high claims to scientific proficiency and its undenominational character, have been chiefly noted. Already six Ph. Ds. and one A. B. *extra ordinem* have been graduated from this University.

Andover Theological Seminary has prepared some Japanese for the ministerial profession.

In Wabash, Ind., Poughkeepsie, N. Y., Parkville, Mo., Colorado Springs, Col., Oberlin, O., and, in short, almost everywhere where there is a college, are to be found the sons of Japan. According to the statistics of 1867 (December 31), there were in the United States 1275 Japanese men and 77 women; 686 of the former and 13 of the latter are recorded as students; 108 and four respectively, as engaged in mercantile vocation.

In general we may say, that there are three classes of students who come to the States. Firstly, such as are sent by the government; these are chosen from among many and are consequently the most promising. Secondly, sons of the wealthy, who are sent by their families for liberal and moral education, and these may make use of their ample means for study or for frivolities. Thirdly, youths with scanty means, but with abundance of ambition, who cross the ocean thoughtlessly and with wild hopes of "making their way," or who with earnestness, and in patience and preservance, acquire knowledge, defying the harsh obstacles set by "chill penury."

The severe conscription laws have driven many a youth to seek some years' shelter in a foreign land, under the pretence of study. As America is so near, a large number have crossed the Pacific solely to evade the military regulations. Hence it is no wonder that the present average intelligence of the Japanese residents in America (as has been noticed by a careful observer, who has been acquainted with our countrymen for several years), is far below what it used to be.

The lowering of the average intelligence of our students in the States, is also due to the fact that, for the past ten years, it has been the policy of the government to send its elect to Europe—especially to Germany. Naturally, the same rage began to prevail among citizens and these now send their children to Germany, in preference to America.

This is not the place to discuss the comparative merits and demerits of giving German or American education to our youths. Such a discussion must necessarily include a survey of the educational and social systems, not only of the two countries, but also of Japan. Moreover, as regards the comparison between Germany and America, a far more competent hand than mine has treated the subject.¹ It is worth while, however, to emphasize for the benefit of our countrymen that, so far as mental training is concerned, the German institutions of learning, as Mr. Hart also says, are far superior to the American. At the same time, the moral influence—and much more the religious—of German academic life, are found wanting when weighed in the balance. If the German education is more thorough, it is at the same time less "wide-awake." In America young men are brought up to make use of what they study, while in Germany they often study until they cannot make use of their knowledge; in other words, the character of American life has necessitated that the education of its young men be practical, while it is also calculated to make well-balanced Christian gentlemen, instead of one-sided specialists in science or philosophy.

From the above, it follows that America is a desirable country to which to send our students of unripe years and with preparation insufficient to pursue clearly defined special branches of study or investigation.

It is doubtful whether it is necessary or desirable, to have so many youths sent to any foreign country without regard to their mental or moral fitness. Even from a financial point of view alone, it is a grave question whether it pays to send a boy of no special talents to Europe or America, at the cost of, say, a thousand dollars a year. There are at least five hundred Japanese students of respectable means, besides several hundreds below comfortable circumstances, studying abroad, for the support of whom at least half a million dollars plus several thousands for travelling expenses, are yearly drained from our poor country. For all this sum, the majority do not acquire any more knowledge than they can at home, if they even obtain so much. The educational facilities in Japan are so great, and living is so moderate, that one can get just as good an education

---

¹ James Morgan Hart, *German Universities*, N. Y. 1874. See especially Pt. II, Chap. VII.

(so far as book-lore is concerned) as in the best American college, for one-fourth or one-fifth of the expense. To make a stay abroad a real educational advantage, one must study and observe actual life in its practical, living issues—and not merely within the narrow walls of a class-room. Without reaping this advantage, a student's foreign sojourn gives him little more than a taste for the luxuries of Western life, and a capital occasion to become denationalized.

Their Mental Aptitudes.

In the choice of studies, the Japanese students have shown a decided inclination to philosophy, law and political economy. Besides the fact of these having been the subject of oriental speculations for ages, in view of the present political and financial reconstruction of our society, many have taken to these studies without judiciously consulting their own special aptitudes. Whatever course of study they may have pursued, however, their records thus far have not been discreditable. On the contrary, in many colleges, prizes and honors have fallen to their lot.

It has frequently been remarked, that, compared with the old system of Japanese rudimentary education, which consisted in cultivating memory at the expense of other discipline, a general collegiate course in America must be to them an easy task, that is so far as class-room recitation is concerned. To present the other side of this view, it has been further remarked that they show no originality. Generalizations of this kind, founded on limited observations, though plausible, are far from being conclusive.

Dr. Charles F. Thwing[1] has well observed in his comparison of Chinese and Japanese students, that the latter are more

---

[1] See his interesting article in *Scribner's Monthly* (old), Vol. XX, p. 450, where he also speaks of Chinese youths being passive, Japanese impulsive, &c. See also a philosophical attempt at the analysis of Japanese character by Mr. Lyman, *Journal of Speculative Philosophy*, Jan. or March, 1886. Mr.

proficient in mathematics and that the former excel in the line of literature. This is but one indication of that singularly analytic character of the people, and is an effect of their exclusively mental training. An analytic mind makes a good scientist, but rarely a practical man; it may make a philosopher, but seldom a statesman. It is prone to be irreligious, radical and destructive. The political and intellectual history of New Japan is a story of continuous destruction of old ideas and institutions; but how little of the elements of the New Régime proceeded from native brains! Even the recent reactionary so-called *national* ideas are, to a great extent, a babbling echo of German Chauvinism. Well may Japanese character be said to be wanting in originality. Here, however, some excuse is to be found in the precipitous haste of our late movements, which left no leisure to thinkers or investigators. Everything was, and is still to a great extent, an experiment or a temporary device in the radical reconstruction of national life. In its eagerness to assimilate Western institutions, Japan has tried to utilize the acquisitions of every young man who has "rubbed himself against a foreigner." Young college graduates have been thrust into positions of high responsibility. They naturally committed errors; but the wonder is that blunders are not more numerous.

Many of those who studied in the States are, or were, connected with the Imperial University. MR. TOYAMA, A. M. of Michigan University, is the Dean of the Literature Faculty. KANDA, educated at Amherst, is Professor of English and Latin. HATAKEYAMA, who studied in Rutgers and who died in 1876, was for many years Director of the University. HATTORI, a Rutgers graduate of 1875, was for a long time Vice-Director. ENOUYE, law graduate of Harvard, filled until his death the chair of Jurisprudence. YAMA-

---

Lyman's conclusions, so far as they go, are ingenious. Had he tried to verify them by historical facts, without which a generalization of national character is a dangerous venture, he would have modified some of his views.

KAWA, Professor of Physics, is a graduate of Yale. YATABE, in charge of the Botanical department, studied in Cornell and Harvard. MITSUKURI, Professor of Biology, KUHARA, lecturer on Chemistry, and MOTORA, lecturer on Philosophy, are Ph. Ds. of the Johns Hopkins University. NAKASHIMA, Ph. D. of Yale, and for some time lecturer in the same institution, is now connected with the University. MURAOKA, a Chemist, studied in Yale and Harvard. PROFESSOR HATOYAMA is a D. C. L. of Yale University.

Among prominent lawyers in government service or in private practice, are KIKUCHI, graduate of Law Department in Boston University, now Private Secretary to the Minister of Justice; MEGATA, Harvard LL. B. of 1874; KANEKO, Harvard LL. B. of 1878, and NAKAYAMA and KURINO, who all studied in the same institution.

In Finance, MR. TAJIRI, graduate of Yale, is in charge of the Bureau of Public Debts. MR. TOMITA, who studied in New York, is at the head of the Banking Bureau. YOSHIWARA, the lamented director of the Bank of Japan was also educated in America. MR. SHIBA, B. F. of the University of Pennsylvania and now the editor of an influential paper, was for some time Private Secretary to the Minister of Agriculture and Commerce.

Among those engaged in religious work was MR. NIISHIMA, one of the first to come to the United States. He studied in Amherst, where he graduated in 1870. Converted to Christianity, he became its worthy champion, and through his college in Saikyo (Kyoto), supported by the American Board for Foreign Missions, he has proved himself a blessing and an honor to his country. ISONAGA, who came to America about 1866 and was afterward naturalized, is said to be a pastor in New England. OGIMI and KIMURA, who studied for about ten years in Holland, Mich., and New Brunswick, are now missionaries of the Reformed Church of America.

In Agriculture, MR. TSUDA is well known, and has been a zealous student of American farming. MR. HASHIGUCHI,

Director of Sapporo College in Hokkaido, graduated from the Massachusetts Agricultural College. Mr. SATO, Vice-Director of the Sapporo College, is a Ph. D. of the Johns Hopkins University. Mr. TAMARI, Professor in the late College at Komaba, was educated in Georgetown and Lansing. MIYABE, now Professor of Botany in Sapporo, is a D. Sc. of Harvard.

Among engineers, now that the railroad fever is at its height, young men who have either studied in Colleges or worked on the field in America, all fill important places. The graduates of Troy Polytechnic Institute, Messrs. MATSUMOTO and HIRAI, fill very responsible positions in government service. Messrs. OBITHA and NOMBURI, for some time in the Penn's R. R. Co., are in positions of trust in northern private railroads. SHIRASHI, who was engaged in active work in Philadelphia and New York, is now Professor of Civil Engineering in the Imperial University. HIROI, C. E, for some time in the service of the Mississippi River Commission, and afterward in Edge Moor Iron Bridge Works, was appointed a Professor of the College in Sapporo.

The above are a few of those who have survived the ordeals of protracted studies. Physically of feebler calibre, their intense application has carried many bright youths to an untimely grave. Thus far, the mortality of our students who have studied abroad, is calculated at forty per cent.—i. e. two in every five! and this at the prime of manhood, say between 26 and 35 years of age.

Morals.

Lest an interested party appear to blow a trumpet, let us here begin with some of the misdemeanors and crimes of the Japanese in the United States. In 1884, in Ogden, Utah, a Japanese who was a waiter in a restaurant quarrelled with the proprietress. On being discharged, he avenged himself by firing at her. The woman died and he was severely condemned by "Judge Lynch." Two years later, in San Francisco, was repeated a similar tragedy, but this time the players were both Japanese. In Washington Territory, in 1886, a Japanese killed a Chinese. "George Taro," accused of homicide in New Jersey in 1887, was subsequently proved to be "not guilty."

Among a few silly incidents, may be mentioned the case of a young man, who, on his way from San Francisco to Boston, found in the train, or rather in his brain, a plan to kidnap him and sell him in Canada for a slave. The distracted youth chose the alternative of risking his life by jumping out of a fast running train, to the sufferings of a slave life in Canada! He was restored to consciousness by a tramp, only to be robbed of what little he had. Another young man, working in Colorado Springs, and afterwards in New York City, behaved improperly, and, having been found upon medical examination to be a monomaniac, he was placed in a New Jersey Asylum, where he died. The suicide of a Secretary of Legation in Washington, was a singular circumstance, of which the cause is not exactly known.

To present another side of the life of Japanese residents in America,—it does credit to the patriotism and training of the youths, that, without the religious restraints of professing Christians and away from home influences, they maintain their integrity and honor. Teetotalers in principle, very few of them are; but a drunken Japanese is an unknown sight in the States. Smoking is a national custom; but that has only a remote connection with morals: the wonder among them is, that a cigar store in America should pander to salacity. Opium smoking is totally unknown among us. The Japanese mind was not "original" enough to conceive so Western a habit as that of snuffing or chewing tobacco, and we know of one new-comer to American shores, who noted in his diary that "the saliva of Americans is dark." Gambling is not even thought of. Swearing—the Japanese language is devoid of a profane vocabulary! Can this be the

reason that some western writers think our language so
defective?

What keeps an average Japanese resident in foreign countries from the ways of the wicked and the foolish, is his strong sense of personal and national honor. "Is it manly?" "Will it disgrace my country's name?" are questions ever kept before him, if he has no higher dictates of religion or morals. One father writes to his son as he takes leave of him for America: "Above all, take it close to thy heart to live worthy of thy country. Remember that thou wilt be thrown amongst strangers of different ideas and customs. With a standard different from that to which thou hast been accustomed, and with a harsher measure, will they mete thee. Every word thou utterest falls not upon indifferent ears; every act of thy hand somebody watches. Should any action of thine dim in the least the lustre of thy country's glory or stain the brightness of thy family's records, then father me no longer father, I will no more son thee my son."

In College towns where there are any number of Japanese, a club is formed where they meet at stated intervals for mutual improvement, moral and intellectual. Letters of friendship or of instructive information pass from club to club.

Since 1886, the Japanese students in the United States, or more exactly on the Atlantic Coast, have formed an Association for the purpose of mutual intercourse. They meet once a year, some time during vacations.

Religion.

As to Religion in any form or with any formula, it has for years been at a discount in Japan. No Japanese, therefore, takes with him to the States any "strange gods." Few, indeed, except those who became Christians at home, come with any definite religious conviction. In America, however, few can long be blind to the existence of a mighty social force in Religion. Even the most superficial tourist has noted that

America is a religious country—if not a country of religion, at least of religionism (to borrow a word from the Bishop of Ripon). To any one who has taken the least pains to see below the surface of the religious life professed by many church members, the impressions are not at first of a favorable nature; for, objectively, the inconsistencies between the profession and the life of many pew-renters, church-goers, etc., are flagrant, and being subjectively a stranger to those experiences which only believers can understand, a Japanese observer of Western religion hastily comes to the conclusion that, since he sees so little that appeals to him as spiritual, it is all mere sham. He goes to Church and finds a rich display of gaudy colors in dress and bonnet, listens to hymns sung apparently without understanding, hears a learned discourse on moral duty, not very different from that which formed part of his instruction as a pagan, or it may be a most commonplace sermon on an antiquated dogmatic theme. All at once a basket is thrust before him, which reminds him that even in this so-called House of Worship, "money changers" must not be wanting. He may occasionally attend prayer-meetings or revivals, and finds himself in the midst of amazing demonstrations, such as he used to associate at home with only the most ill-balanced minds.

In view of these unfavorable impressions, it is not surprising, though it is to be greatly regretted, that many a bright and earnest mind which embraced Christianity in Japan, is disappointed, even disgusted, and not unfrequently gives up its faith to find a more rational belief in Philosophy or Science.

It is also to be lamented that not a few Christian Japanese, on coming to the States and finding their religious profession so respected and respectable, fall easy victims to superficial piety, at the sacrifice of the spiritual vigor which comes with struggle. On the contrary, those who have embraced Christianity under hot-bed influences of American church life, can poorly endure transplanting to the more chilling atmosphere of paganism and unbelief, to which they must be exposed on their return home. The budding faith of such is apt to wither at the first blast of infidelity.

We have spoken above of bad impressions of American religionism. These are only more and more confirmed, until the observer perceives through the intimacy of personal intercourse, that, in spite of prevailing counterfeits, there are many genuine, devoted Christian lives in closest relationship with their Master. Or, it may be that he realizes (without knowing such) that, were American religion only mere show, there must be some basis for its "big pretensions." Whichever of these thoughts may lead our Japanese to the study of Christianity and possibly to conversion, the process is generally from without inward—growing from the surface, the outermost manifestations of Christianity, gradually inward towards the central figure of Christ—a process essentially analytic. They must investigate before they can believe; thus they unconsciously conform to the biblical precept—" Prove all things." In such investigations, the conflicting tenets of the countless sects of this country, must be duly scrutinised and weighed. This they do fearlessly, being bound by no tradition or church interests. The dry, logical method of research, without fear of consequence, oft lands the seeker in a miry slough of despond (Agnosticism), or upon the ethereal height of Christian intellectualism (Unitarianism), or in the mystic depth of spiritual Christianity (Quakerism).

Romance.

From Religion to Romance is quite a jump; but few things are more closely connected than the altar and the sacrament of marriage.

When wedlock has occurred in the United States, the wooed party was the American, and when in Japan, the reverse. A few students have taken home American brides, and a former Secretary of our Legation obtained a Baltimorean for his companion in life. Some resident merchants in New York have

Caucasian wives, while some half-dozen jugglers, wrestlers and artisans have won the affection of Yankee girls.

Love disregards the rules of grammar, and, notwithstanding the difficulty with which the husbands in many cases manage a foreign language, they and their wives are, to all appearances, living happily.

Instances of marriage between American women and Japanese men are rarer than those of German Mädchen and our countrymen. The most prominent example of the latter is that of Mr. Aoki, our present Minister of Foreign Affairs, who married a German baroness. A few of the professors in the University and some officials in high positions, have also European wives.

If experience thus far has not been conducive to the encouragement of intermarriage between Japanese and Americans, the reason is to be sought elsewhere than solely in the intermixture of blood. Such marriages as those of a juggler and a servant girl, or of a man of questionable character and a woman of no better reputation, cannot afford any satisfaction, entirely apart from any race differences. Ethnology, to pass a rational judgment, must wait for better examples.

Lately, much sense, and more nonsense, have seen the light through the Japanese press, on the subject of improving the race. Among manifold means suggested, the desirability of an intermixture of Caucasian blood has been hotly debated. Into the general scientific considerations of the subject we shall not enter, as even the best authorities are divided thereon. It is a dangerous expedient to encourage wedlock on a patriotic or scientific ground. It takes two—no more, no less—to marry; and so the decision must be left to them. At the same time, it is a mere truism to state that the parties concerned must possess clear knowledge of the conditions under which their life is to be passed. Of these conditions, the most formidable are the difference in language and the difference in the standards of living. The former can be conquered after a few years' residence, while the difficulties of the latter largely

depend upon the financial status of the parties. All other so-
called difficulties and obstacles—different manners and customs
—are comparatively of inferior magnitude. Even the lower
social position which woman occupies in Japan, affects the
foreign-born Japanese wives far less than the native-born.

The magnitude of the difficulties, however, is more subjec-
tive than objective, and it dwindles into insignificance, when
the parties concerned find congeniality in mutual intellectual
enjoyments and are bound by the all-conquering bond of love,
sanctified by a common faith. Without unity in spiritual
affairs, the best marriage may share the fate of Robert and
Catharine Elsmere's.

Female Students.

History and literature amply show that the status of our
women in past times was far better than at present or in times
of Feudalism; that their position was lowered in consequence
of the introduction of Buddhism and Confucianism, the latter
of which despises the gentle sex as deficient in intelligence,
and the former as abounding in sin.

Doubtless there is truth in Herbert Spencer's theory in
regard to the influence of militarism upon the position of
women. In a society where men are especially honored as
the defenders of the battle-field and the strength of a nation,
women naturally sink to a lower plane, and so we find our
mothers and sisters becoming less powerful factors in the
national life, during the days of Feudalism and the Shogunate. This idea seems to be verified, even in the relative freedom enjoyed by the three classes which form the bulk of our
nation. Women of the lower or industrial class have the
greatest degree of liberty, corresponding to what Mr. Spencer
says of the condition of women in an industrial Society.
Among the Samurai, or military class, she has least personal
freedom, illustrating what has been said above. In the circle
of the nobility, whose occupations consisted mostly of indoor
and literary pursuits, the seclusion of their life and their con-

sequent need of fit companionship, gave to the women of their households much the same importance as was ascribed to them in the courts of the European suzerains of the Middle ages, as spoken of by M. Guizot. For example, it may be stated here that much of our classical literature was written by court ladies.

Again, we believe that the lack of education on the part of our women, is not so much due to their supposed inherent incapacity and the lower position assigned them, as that their position is due to the lack of a more liberal education, which, in turn, may be attributed to their inferior status under militarism.

The elevation of the status of woman, begun since the New Régime, is not, therefore, merely an assimilation of Western ideas, but a revival of old national ideas, and, as such, is doubly laudable.

Seeing that many young men were fast advancing in western education and that they—"the lords of creation"—were acquiring an undue proportion of intelligence, it was thought desirable that young women should likewise receive western education, in order to become efficient companions for the youths. Educational institutions were established without number. But not till the government took the initiative, did any woman venture abroad, except a few singing or dancing girls who accompanied acrobatic troops and the like. The Colonial Department (Kaitakushi, now defunct), at the instance of General Kuroda, proposed in its scheme of education, to send, on its own account, a few girls of well-known families to be educated in the United States.[1] The young Emperor and his Consort cordially acquiesced in the proposal, and, in 1871, was signed the edict which ran: "My country is now undergoing a complete change from old to new ideas, which I sincerely desire; therefore, I call upon all the wise

---

[1] For details, see Lanman, *Japanese in America*.

and strong-minded to appear and become good guides to the Government. During youthtime it is positively necessary to view foreign countries, so as to become enlightened as to the ideas of the world; and boys, as well as girls, who will themselves become men and women, should be allowed to go abroad, and my country will be benefited by their knowledge so acquired. Women, therefore, have had no position socially, because it was considered that they were without understanding; but if educated and intelligent they should have due respect. Five young Japanese women of rank go to America in care of Mrs. De Long, to be sent to some seminary of learning at the expense of the government." The girls referred to were Misses YOSHIMATSU, age fifteen, WUYEDA, fifteen, YAMAKAWA, twelve, NAGAI, ten, and TSUDA, eight. When their arrival in the States was known, numerous applications were made by educational institutions to take them in charge. They were for some time placed in Georgetown, D. C., under the general supervision of Mr. and Mrs. Lanman, the youngest being made a member of their household, where she remained for more than ten years, until her return. Two were sent home after a short time. Two studied in Vassar, one graduating with some honor. All except the youngest have since married. Miss Tsuda has now returned to America and is studying in Bryn Mawr College. Besides these wards of government, a few other young women studied in different parts of the Union.

As we have said in speaking of young men, it is not worth the trouble or expense on the part of the Government to send abroad unprepared students—youths or maidens—only to denationalize them, as is apt to be the case when they leave their native land at too early an age; therefore, we think it was wisely concluded not to continue such experiments, without a definite object clearly in view. For, while we warmly advocate for woman, as for man, thorough and liberal education, we deplore methods which are in themselves so radical as to be revolutionary and denationalizing. Between the kitchen and the platform lie many phases of gradual development, else one must ignore both intellectual and moral foundations, in the leap from the one to the other. The nineteenth century, even in its advanced decades, has found woman in Japan still occupying the sphere of the kitchen (or at best that of the parlor), and this without a knowledge of principles, which, when put into practice there, elevate her from drudgery into the field of science. Let her, we would plead, for the sake of her own true development and the healthier moral and physical life of those who come under her influence as husbands and children, first apply herself to household sciences in their manifold branches, to a better knowledge of the laws which govern her own being and the minds and bodies of those about her; in a word, to all that ennobles, beautifies and makes more healthful the home, and through it strengthens the moral fibre of the nation. Only when its forces for growth and usefulness radiate from the home and are strongly centred there, does oriental or occidental womanhood step from the social problems of the inside to those of the outside world. Our women need to realize this more fully, in their eager desire for rapid development—even more fully do those who wish to help them attain it, need to realize it.

Lately (1885), the Government has sent out a young lady to the States, but this time with a definite work assigned her. MISS KIN KATO came to Salem, Mass., under the auspices of the Educational Department, to study the normal school and kindergarten systems. Also, MISS NOBU KODA has recently been sent to the Boston Conservatory of Music.

Two young ladies, MISS YASO HISHIKAWA and MRS. KEI NISHIDA OKAMI, studied medicine; the former in Chicago and the latter in Philadelphia. Upon her return, Mrs. Okami was placed in charge of the woman's department in the Charity Hospital at Tokyo. In the Western Maryland College, Westminster, Md., studies one MISS MASAO TSUNE HIRATA; in Mt. Holyoke, MISS MIYAKAWA. A MRS. TAMURA came to New York State, to learn the necessary duties of a pastor's wife. All these ladies are more or less connected with Christian missions. In the Pacific University, Cal., Miss Soso has taken a course in law, and on her return she expects, it is said, to be an attorney. Besides them, there are in Washington, D. C., Chambersburg and Overbrook, Pa., San Francisco and Oakland, Cal., several young ladies at school.

Japanese in California.

In 1870, there came to San Francisco eleven Japanese from Hawaii, who settled in the City in various capacities. Until 1880, the number of the Japanese in the City amounted to about two hundred. The promulgation of compulsory conscription laws, suddenly increased the emigration of youths who are loath to serve in the army. Those whose parents can afford it, are generally sent to Europe, while those who have to fight their own battles flock to the Golden State. The movement is encouraged by Mr. Fukuzawa, who preaches through his paper to the young men, with the authoritative voice of a Horace Greeley, bidding them "go west."[1] Consequently the growth of population in San Francisco has lately been steady and rapid. In 1883, there were about 150, in 1884 the number doubled, in 1885 there were 557, and early the next year about 800. In the fall of 1887, there were some 2,000, whereas, in the beginning of 1889, about 500 new-comers were added; and at present nearly 3,000 must be living in California. They are spread in many parts of the State, but their favorite resorts are San Francisco, Alameda and Oakland, the greatest number naturally flocking to the first named city, where it is said there is a whole street almost exclusively occupied by them.[2]

These Japanese in California range generally from 18 to 30 years in age, and represent by no means the laboring

---

[1] "West," "Western Ocean," "Western nation," in common speech, signifies among the Japanese, America and Europe.
[2] Cf. Japan Weekly Mail, March 8, 1890.

classes. Many of them are the sons of old samurai, full of ambition and energy, yet without means to obtain a liberal education.

As to their means of subsistence, there are very few who are professional men or who are mere drudges. There are two Japanese physicians practising in San Francisco. Law students are debarred by statute from pleading in the State courts. Very few Japanese names are to be found in the college catalogues of the State. There is, however, an instructor of Chinese and Japanese languages, in the Maclay Institute of Theology at San Fernando.

The majority—we might say nearly all—of the Japanese in California, make their living as waiters, domestics, and shopboys, while the stronger serve as sailors or coasters. It is usual with many of them to make an arrangement with their employers, by which they are allowed an hour or two each day, in order to attend schools; this of course at the sacrifice of their wages. One cannot too much admire the pluck of some of the boys, who, laboring under unaccustomed disadvantages, are still ambitious to carry home the learning of the West. It is only to be hoped that many will have such aspirations.

Unfortunately, however, in such a large conglomerate community, there is sure to be a leaven of dissatisfaction and mischief. This found its vent from time to time in a little paper published among them. "Jiuku-Seiki" (the Nineteenth Century), published at San Francisco, proved so objectionable that it came under censure of the press in Japan. Under another name "Ji-yu" (Liberty), the paper is still continued.

The moral and educational advantages of San Francisco are far from being satisfactory, and it is with fear and trembling that one watches the lively influx thither of our youths and maidens. Respecting the latter, the record book of arrivals at the port shows eighty-eight names of women, inscribed during the twelve months of 1889. Thirty are stated to be domestics, another thirty tourists and students, three seamstresses,

one nurse and one teacher. Several of them might simply
have passed through the port, but there is strong suspicion as
to the real vocation of some of these women.

To give the young men advantages of moral education, has
been the attempt of many earnest christian workers of the city.
Dr. and Mrs. Gibson, of the Methodist Episcopal Church,
have sheltered many a Japanese youth in connection with the
Chinese mission. Lately, Mr. M. C. Harris, for eleven years
a missionary in Japan, has taken up the work, and a Japanese mission has been organized in Oakland and San Francisco.
His wife, notwithstanding her delicate health, devotes all her
strength and energy to the cause of what she calls "her adopted
country" (Japan). There is also a Presbyterian mission among
the Japanese. Some benevolent Christian ladies, seeing that
ignorance of any handiwork among the young men is in the
way of their securing good positions, have established cookery-
schools and similar institutions for them.[1]

It is not unlikely that the Japanese population in the
West will increase slowly. The people show little migratory instinct, even within their own country; they have been
altogether too stationary. Within recent times, however, we
have seen several hundreds emigrating to the Sandwich Islands,
at the request of the government of Hawaii. Thence to America is an easy and pleasant change. One usually reliable
paper[2] writes in 1884 (but with how much truth it is hard to
say), that, "within the last few months, over 200 peasants or
petty farmers have left Japan to settle in the Western States,
and it is more than probable that their example will be followed by large numbers. . . . America," it continues, "is
to be congratulated on these adjuncts to Western industry.
The Japanese peasants are as industrious as they are frugal,

---

[1] Mr. Tompkins of Oakland, Cal., has made a gift of $50,000 to the State
University there, to be devoted to the encouragement of studies in Chinese
and Japanese.
[2] *The Bradstreet's*, Oct. 25, 1884.

temperate and skilled." And, so long as they do not really come in numbers, the Americans may congratulate themselves on these "adjuncts;" but when once Japanese labor enters the market, may it not, like Chinese, become an object of exclusion policy? Already there are heard voices, which extend the interpretation of the nineteenth article of the Constitution of California, claiming that it is intended to cover not only the Chinese but the Japanese, that is the "Mongolian" race, as section second of the said article puts it. Again, in section fourth, the word "Asiatic coolieism" is used, which may involve the Japanese laborer.

Exhibitions, Mercantile Houses, &c.

Of exhibitions, first in importance was the Centennial, which, as has already been said, formed an epoch in the commercial relations between the United States and Japan, and in the introduction of Japanese art into the Union. It was at once an advertisement of Japanese wares and of the capabilities of Japanese industry. As it was so different from the exhibits of other nations, the Japanese department, it is said, attracted the largest number of visitors. The Japanese commissioners did not fail to show where we stood—not only in art, but in education and general culture. In the later exhibition of 1883, in Boston, Japanese exhibits were sold to a large amount and several prizes were awarded to them. In the Cotton Exhibition of St. Louis also, Japan gained no small share of general attention and admiration.

Many Japanese troops of various kinds have passed through the States from time to time,—acrobats, wrestlers, and what not. More recently, what are known as Japanese Villages have been on exhibition in nearly all principal towns of the Union, and are said to represent the arts of Japan. Shows of this kind are likely to give more misconceptions than just ideas of Japanese life. The artists or artisans themselves are rarely a representative class. The walled six-feet-square booths they erect, are very often taken by thoughtless observers as reproductions of native dwellings. Women who shamefacedly expose themselves in these exhibitions, are, in American democratic parlance, called "ladies," and are taken as types of matrons and daughters of the Sunrise Kingdom.

The Japanese firms in American cities date from the Centennial Exhibition. New York is naturally the City where they have their centers. The *First Japanese Manufacturing and Trading Co.*, established in 1877, is in a prosperous condition, doing a business of some $150,000 in its retail department and of some $100,000 more in the wholesale. The *Nippon Mercantile Co.*, was started a little later and deals only in wholesale business. *Morimura & Bros.*, a wholesale firm, has a well-known store in Broadway. Another firm of well-grounded reputation in New York City, is the *Kan Sai Trading Co.*, which likewise has its agency in Broadway. The *Doshin Silk Co.* has its agency in New York, where it deals in raw silk. Started soon after the Centennial Exhibition, with a subsidy from the government, it has constantly grown in importance. It is one of the few companies which is engaged in direct export trade.

In San Francisco, there are a half-dozen stores under the management of the Japanese, where their country's productions are sold; but these are mostly of recent establishment and of little importance, except *Okri* and *Nishimura*. For about two years after the fall of 1884, the *Ichi Ban* in San Francisco — the *Nee Ban* of Chicago — an American firm, was in full operation for the purpose of exhibiting and selling Japanese wares, and disseminating a knowledge of Japanese arts and manufactures.

Among smaller Japanese concerns in several towns of the Union, the one in Baltimore — *Nonaka & Co.* — commonly known among the towns-people as a "real Japanese store," is doing a successful business of some $17,000 a year.

Of inestimable help to these houses, as well as to the cause of American-Japanese commerce, have been the Agencies in San Francisco and New York, of the *Yokohama Specie Bank*. These Agencies were established in 1881; but not till 1884 could they open any direct negotiation with American houses, since which time they have naturally increased in utility, credit and transactions.

Lastly, a few words on Japanese contributions to America. Can any good come out of a heathen land?—Good or bad, many articles that add to the pleasures of life more than to its necessities, have been the contributions of Japan to the United States. Of silk and tea, it is needless to speak, neither of fans and parasols.[1] Our paper[2] and soy are becoming more common. A large number of plants, mostly for ornamental purposes, has been introduced. A few of the principal are the clematis, pœonies, magnolias, wistarias, Camellia (Japonica), tea-plant, maples, cherries, hydrangeas, chrysanthemums, nandia, kerria, rhododendrons, persimmons, pawlownia imperialis, daphne, ginko, pines, iris, lilies, &c., &c. In the world of female fashion, certain forms of a broad sash tied behind in a large bow; of a collar crossing upon the breast, somewhat like the so-called surplice dress of the day, and a narrow, short, straight bang, are attributed to Japanese influences. That novel form of book-binding in which the cord is shown on the covers, now so common in gift books, is a Japanese contribution to Western bibliopegy. The idea of ornamenting book-covers with flower-stalks or with some other bold, dashy strokes of suggestive effect, is likewise of Japanese importation. In fact, innumerable designs in dress and art are of Japanese origin. Whether in painting in its

---

[1] Soon after the Perry Expedition, a paper parasol of the quality that now costs fifty cents, was, it is said, sold at ten dollars!

[2] In the Surgical Dep't., University of Pennsylvania, Dr. Roberts uses Japanese paper as towels for drying wounds, while it is quite valuable as a substitute for cotton in dentistry.

various forms—from the humorous sketches of sumi-ye and toba-ye, to the sedate and graceful productions of the Kano and Tosa schools; or in Karunies—Owari, Satsuma, Kaga and others; or in embroidery or cloisonné (shippō), or in lacquer ware or bronze work—Japanese art has stamped its influence upon Europe and America to an extent everywhere appreciable; so much so that the *London Times*[1] expressed the belief that Tokyo will become the capital of the artistic world. Whatever may be the artistic future of Tokyo, this much seems to be sure — that the unique and extensive collections of lacquer ware by Dr. Bigelow, of pictures by Professor Fenellosa, and of pottery by Professor Morse, show the promise of the near future that Boston, not content to be the center of the world, is to become the center of Japanese art outside of Japan.

While art products are imported in large quantities from Japan into the States, the artistic taste of the Japanese is little known and less shared by the Americans. Nothing is more revolting to our idea of good taste than the "loud," mixed colors of the dress worn in the opera of the "Mikado." The decoration of rooms with all sorts of bric-à-brac, fans and panels, which is said to be Japanese taste, is most strangely alien to it. Even the house of the wealthiest or the most artistic in Japan, is cold and bare compared with an American drawing-room. The well known artist, Mr. John La Farge, writing from Japan says: "It is possible that when I return I shall feel still more distaste for the barbarous accumulations in our houses, and recall the far more civilized emptiness persisted in by the more æsthetic race."[2]

Farewell.

What began must end. An odious law is this, when one is not quite ready for the end. The sons of Japan studying in the States feel this odium, when after three, four or five

---

[1] 25 January, 1888.   [2] *The Century Magazine*, June, 1890, p. 222.

years' stay, they must go home to enter an active life, for which they may not be prepared. After a residence of perhaps four years, in a country where one has to use a different language—where he passes most of his time with books and within the walls of academic buildings—where all the while he comes in contact (generally speaking) with only one set of people; namely, "young fellows" who are often as green as himself—where rarely he is received into the intimacy of a family—where he can seldom make bosom friends—where his racial conspicuousness prevents him from peeping into the nooks and corners of American life, even if it be merely for observation's sake—where social oppression prevents one from free movement—where to be an oriental "heathen," is to be generally despised by more heathenish (uncultured) masses; after years spent under conditions involving so many disadvantages, he finds that he has just tasted the rind, bitter or sweet, of the fruit of American life. It may be, however, that life in America has not tasted particularly sweet or particularly bitter; it may have been insipid.

As a young graduate casts his last fond look upon the college buildings and the campus, and home-bound sails cast across the Atlantic, or journeys west across the prairies; as he tries to fix in his memory incidents of his life in America, he finds that life as devoid of variety or interest as the waste of waters or of land through which he travels.

Let him meditate a little longer, then will there rise before him individual forms of men, women and children, noble, serene and fair, who in gentlest voice will say,—"While you were among us, our doors were ever open to welcome you. Our hands were always extended to receive you. We were only too glad and ready to cheer your life among strangers. But, whether it was from difficulty in language or considerations of courtesy, you kept yourself aloof from us. Now that you leave our land, our kind wishes and prayers go with you. Farewell!" Then for the first time he realizes that he has neglected great and

rare opportunities for practical education—education in its
noblest sense; then comes thronging back upon his memory
every offer of willing help from his teacher which he has not
accepted,—every gracious act of his friends which he has not
appreciated,—every Christian doctrine which he has not
examined, and every encouragement to higher intellectual
and moral life which America gives to each aspiring soul, but
to which he has only feebly responded. All that his lips can
now utter, gushes from the inmost recesses of his newly
awakened heart, and in grateful accents echoes back

FAREWELL.!

INDEX.

[The letter "J" stands for Japan or Japanese.]

A.

Adams, J. Quincy, interest in J., 32.
Adams, Wm., in J., 17.
Agnosticism in J., 130.
Agriculture, American service to J., 134–137.
America, J. in, 3, 4, 157–191; treaty of, with Korea, 5; attempts to open J., 31–42; sends Perry, 42; trade with J., 90–96; friendly diplomacy, 96; influence of, on J., 110–156; writers of, on J., 141–151.
Amherst College, 167.
Andover Seminary, 167.
Antisell, Dr., 134.
Aoki, Viscount, 107.
Ap Jones, D. W., 136.
Aulick, Com., mission to J., 41.

B.

Belgium, J. treaty with, 104.
Berry, Dr. J. C., 156.
Biddle, Com., visit to J., 33, 38.
Bingham, J. A., service to J., 97, 98; on Capron, 135, 136.
Black Ship, song of, 1.
Blaine, James G., receives J. Embassy, 104.
Blake, Wm. P., 133.
Boutwell, Geo. S., 116.
Brooks, Wm. P., 136.
Brown, Dr. S. R., 132.
Bryan, Sam. M., postal service of, 127.
Bryce, on American diplomacy, 68, 108.

C.

Buchanan, Pres., reception of J. Embassy, 100.
Buckle, Thomas, 110.
Buckley, Mrs., 126.
Burrows, S. R., service in J., 62.

California, J. in, 168–184.
Canoes on J., 6.
Capron, Gen., in J. service, 133.
Caron, memorial on J., 34.
Carrothers, Mrs. J. D., firm-film Kingdom, 146.
Cassell, Com., 130.
Catharine II, interest in J., 22.
Cecil, Lord Eustace, on J., 152.
Cadille, Admiral, visits J., 34.
Chaplin, W. A., 123.
Charlevoix on Christian persecutions, 13.
China, intercourse with J., 6; influence of, 6, 20.
Chiwata in Yeso, 32.
Chamblin, daimio of, 61.
Christian persecutions in J., 11.
Clark, E. W., life in J., 143.
Clark, Col. Wm. S., in J. service, 136.
Cocks, Richard, residence in J., 16.
Codilla, Chas. C., travels in J., 144.
Colhurt, interest in J., 34.
Columbia Univ., 167.
Columbus, writes to J. Emperor, 7.
Commercial treaty, 66.
Cooper, Capt., visits J., 32.
Cooper, Peter, 113.
Cornell Univ., 160.

Cotton trade, 75, 91.
Crawford, J. U., in J. service, 138.
Currency question, 71.
Curtius, Donker, 55.
Cutter, Dr. J. C., 122, 126.

D.

Daukichi, 76, 158.
Daté sends mission to Rome, 15.
Davidoff in Yesso, 23.
DeLong, Chas. E., 88, 163.
Denison, Mr., 139.
DePauw Univ., 166.
Derby, Capt., arrives in J., 31.
Deshima, foreign colony in, 20.
Devereux, arrival in J., 31.
Doty comes to J., 63.

E.

Eastlake, Dr. F. W., 140.
Echizen, memorial of, 82.
Education, American influence in, 116–123.
Elgin, Lord, 151.
Eliot, Chas. W., 118.
Ellesmere, Earl of, on J., 44.
England, intercourse with J., 16.
Enouye, Count, 105.
Enouye, 171.
Exclusion policy in J., 13, 24.
Exhibitions, J., in America, 186.
Extradition treaty, 100.

F.

Female, J., students in America, 179–183.
Fenollosa, Prof., on art, 122.
Ferris, Dr. J. M., on J. students, 165.
Feudalism, moral effects of, 152.
Field, H. M., on J., 145.
Fillmore, Pres., on J. expedition, 38, 46.
Fisher on J. currency, 74.
Foote, Gen., in Corea, 99.
France, intercourse with J., 24.
Fukuchi, 163.
Fukuzawa, school, 117, 119; encourages emigration, 183.

G.

Gainfield, J. A., 118.
German educational influence, 169.
Gibson, Dr., 185.
Gilman, D. C., on indemnity, 87.
Glynn, Capt., visits J., 36; his service, 39, 41.
Goble, Mr., 140, 158.
Golownin, capture of, 23.
Grant, Gen., on Bingham, 97; on American policy in J., 99; visits J., 140; account of his travels, 146.
Greey, Edward, on J., 146.
Gregorian calendar adopted in J., 129.
Gregory XIII, 15.
Griffis, W. E., on foreign influences in J., 111; writes Readers, 122; Mikado's Empire, 145, 146; on Iwakura, 165.
Gubbins on Christian persecutions, 13.
Guizot, M., 110, 180.
Gutzlaff, Dr., visits J., 32.

H.

Hakodate, foreign trade of, 71; prices in, 75.
Hale, E. E., on Perry Expedition, 62.
Harris, Townsend, advent of, 64; his treaty, 65; on rise of prices, 75; departure from J., 77; on treaty revision, 107; in Yedo, 113–115; compared with Perry, 115–116.
Harris, Mr. and Mrs. M. C., 185.
Hart on German education, 169.
Harvard Univ., 166.
Harwell, Dr., 126.
Hashikura sent to Rome, 15.
Hashiguchi, 172.
Hatakeyama, 171.
Hatoyama, 172.
Hattori, 171.
Hawks, Dr., works on J., 143.
Heco, Joseph, 158.
Heeren, 110.
Heine, Wm., on J., 143.
Henry, Prof. J., 87, 118.
Hepburn, Dr., 121, 122, 126.
Heusken, assassination of, 76.
Hideyoshi, Christian persecutions under, 12.

Hildreth, Rich., on Perry Expedition, 61; on J., 162.
Hill, G. W., 132.
Hirado, foreign trade in, 9, 13, 22.
Hirai, 172.
Hirata, Miss, 162.
Hirai, 172.
Hishihara, Miss, 162.
Hokkaido, Yezo done in, 26; agriculture of, 120.
Holland, intercourse with J., 20; services of, 64, 22.
Horton, 70.
Humu, E. H., represents U. S. government, 97; on missionaries, 121, 123, 124; his journalistic work, 140; works on J., 147, 148.
Hyogo, see Kobe.

I.

Ii-Kamon, assassination of, 76.
Imanga, 172.
Italy, treaty with J., 64.
Iwakura Embassy, 102-166.
Iyeyasu, Christian persecutions under, 11; encourages Adams, 17; latitude of power, 88.

J.

James, L. L., 121, 157.
Japan, intercourse with Korea, 4; with China, 5; with Portugal, 7; Spain, 9; Christian persecutions in, 11; intercourse with England, 16; with Holland, 20; with Russia, 22; with France, 24; isolation of, 15, 24; western knowledge in, 26; in the middle of this century, 28; even after Perry's departure, 62; treaty with Italy and Belgium, 64; changes since Restoration, 68; trade with America, 90-93; friendly diplomacy with U. S., 93-100; American influence in, 110-134; American writers on, 141-151.
Japanese in America, 157-191; their mental aptitude, 170-173; morals, 173-175; religion, 175-177; romance, 177-179; female students, 179-182; in California, 182-186.

Jewett, F. F., 122.
Johns Hopkins Univ., 157.
Johnson, Lieut., on Kanagawa, 60; on J., survey, 72.
Jui-gumi, 22, 23, 181.

K.

Kämpfer on Christian persecutions, 12.
Kanagawa, treaty of, 88; Johnson on, 60.
Kanda, 171.
Kaneko, 172.
Kato, Miss, 162.
Kido, 163.
Kikuchi, 172.
Kimura, 172.
King, Mr., arrival to J., 62; his book, 141.
Kobe-Hyogo, growth of, 72.
Koda, Miss, 162.
Korea, intercourse with J., 4; treaty with U. S., 6; Americans in, 60.
Kubota, 172.
Kurino, 172.
Kuroda, Gen., in Korea, 6; interest in female education, 121; Gov. of Yezo, 126.
Kurile Islands, exchanged for Saghalien, 34.
Kyoto (Saikyo) Jesuits in, 11; imperial court in, 20.

L.

La Farge, letters from J., 144.
Lanman, Chas., on hadsumbry, 97; on J., 148, 149, 181.
Laxman, Lieut., 22.
Le Gendre, Gen., 120, 147.
Leland, Dr., 127.
Lowell, Percival, on J., 149, 150.
Lyman, B. S., 122, 179.

M.

Mackay, A. C., on J., 145.
Maria Louisa case, 133.
Mason, L. W., 130.
Matsuoka, 179.

McCartee, Mr., 139.
McDonald, R., 37, 117.
Megata, 172.
Mendenhall, T. C., 125.
Mercantile Houses, J., 187.
Michelet, M., on whale, 38.
Michigan Univ., 166.
Missions, Christian, 128–134.
Mito, Prince of, 25, 29, 49.
Mitsukuri, Dr., 172.
Miyabe, Dr., 173.
Miyakawa, Miss, 182.
Mori, Arinori, on indemnity, 87; interest in education, 119; on Iwakura Embassy, 163.
Morrison, rumor of his visit to J., 26, 32.
Morse, G. S., scientific services of, 124; literary work on J., 149.
Munroe, Mr., 124.
Muraoka, 172.
Murray, David, 118, 120.
Mutsu, 100.

N.

Nakahama, 47, 157.
Nakashima, 172.
Nakayama, 172.
Nagasaki, opened for foreign trade, 9; western learning in, 25; its decline, 70, 71; prices in, 75.
Nagato, see Choshin.
Niigata, foreign trade in, 71.
Niishima, 172.
Nobechi, 173.
Nobunaga, Christian persecution under, 10.
Normal education, 120.
Northrop, G. B., 87, 88, 118.

O.

Okami, Dr., 182.
Ogimi, 172.
Okubo, 163, 164, 166.
Okuma, Count, 105, 106.
Opium War, 64.
Osaka, Adams in, 17.
Oshima, 173.

P.

Palmer, A. H., interest in J., 39, 40; 144.
Parker, Peter, visit to J., 32; his book, 142.
Paul, H. M., 125.
Peabody, C. H., 136.
Pembroke claim, 79.
Penhallow, D. P., 136.
Perinchief, O., 118.
Perry, Com., foreign intercourse of J. before, 3; his American predecessors, 31; life of, 42; comments on his Expedition, 43; voyage, 45; in Yedo Bay, 46; second visit to J., and treaty, 52–56; Siebold on, 57; his presents to J., 112; Williams on, 113, 115; compared with Harris, 115–116; narrative of his Expedition, 143.
Petroleum, importation into J., 96.
Philadelphia, Japanese in, 161, 167.
Philolethes on J., 142.
Pinto visits J., 7.
Polo, Marco, on J., 7.
Pontiane, Adm., in J., 51, 59.
Porter, Com., plans expedition to J., 31; W. D., on American-Japanese trade, 90.
Portugal, intercourse with J., 7.
Postal system, J., 126–128.
Pratt, Zadoc, interest in J., 33.
Pruyn, Mrs., on J., 145; R. H., minister to J., 77, 78, 79, 83.
Pumpelly, R., 123, 144.

R.

Rai, Sanyo, history of, 30.
Railways, American, 112. 137, 138.
Reed, Mr., comes to J., 63; Sir Edward, on J., 145.
Rein, Prof., on Shimonoseki bombardment, 81.
Religious influence in J., 128–134.
Resanoff, 23.
Restoration of imperial authority, 84.
Rice, W. S., 163.
Richards, Miss, 121.
Richardson affair, 80.
Risley, Mr., 137.

Roberts, Ed., mission to J., 32.
Robertson, 79.
Ronin, outrages of, 77.
Russia, intercourse with J., 72.
Rutgers College, 162.

S.

Sapballos, exchange of, 24, 61.
Saigo, Gen., 164.
Sakuma Shozan, 77.
Sao Park, 157.
Sapporo College, 162.
Savin, Capt., in J., 19.
Seon, Dr., 172.
Sbamons, Friars of, 60; Dominicans
 in, 11.
Scientific services of Americans, 129–
 132.
Scott, Matthew, 129; M. M., 130.
Seelye, Pres., on indemnity, 97.
Seward, Sec., on Imperial Restoration, 64; on indemnity, 92; asked
 to mediate between Russia and J.,
 97; on American influence in J.,
 116, 117; travels of, 144.
Seymour, Sir G., helps Perry, 46.
Shiba, 172.
Shimabara, Catholic revolt of, 13, 21.
Shimmi Embassy to U. S., 150.
Shimoda, opened for foreign trade, 52.
Shimonoseki bombardment, 81; indemnity, 86.
Shiraishi, 172.
Shogun at his wit's end, 46, 77–79;
 fall of, 84; embassy of, 159.
Shoyer, Mr., 79.
Siebold, Archiv., 46; on Perry, 37;
 on J., 52.
Silk, trade in, 75, 81, 95.
Simmons, Dr., 132.
Sinfu, expedition to J., 5.
Smith, E. P., 132.
Soltero on Christian persecution,
 12.
Soon, Miss, 162.
Spain, intercourse with J., 9.
Spalding, J. W., on Perry, 61; on J.
 trade, 60; on J., 142.
Spencer, Herbert, 162, 179.
Stearns, Mr., 79; Wm. A., 118.
Stein, Lorenz von, on treaty revision,
 160.
Stevens, D. W., 139.

Stewart, Capt., comes to J., 31.
Stirling, Adm., in J., 52.
Sundays observed in J., 128.

T.

Taiko, see Hideyoshi.
Tattri, 173.
Talmsge Chapel, 92.
Tamari, 172.
Tammon, Mrs., 132.
Tariff Convention, 64, 68.
Taylor, Bayard, on J., 142, 163; Dr.
 W., 132.
Tea, importation into U. S., 91, 94.
Terry, Prof., 132, 139.
Thwing, Dr., on J. students, 178.
Tilley, H. A., on rise of yedos, 72.
Tokyo, Freemasons in, 11; Dutch
 studies in, 25; Shogun's court in,
 29; imperial cap. in, 98; T. Harris in, 112–115.
Townes, Dr., on J., 144.
Tomita, 172.
Tuyama, 171.
Trade, American-Japanese, 68.
Treat, U., 132.
Treaty, Perry's, 52–59; Dutch proposal of, 66; Harris', 68; extradition, 100; revision of, 152–160.
Tronson, voyage to J., 30; on J.
 bazaar, 91.
Tsuda, 172; Miss, 181.
Tycoon, see Shogun.

U.

Uraga, Perry in, 47, 48.

V.

Van Buren, Thos., on labor in J., 147.
Verder, Mr., 132.
Vehicle on Christian persecution,
 12.
Verbeck, Dr., on Protestant missions,
 132; services of, 179, 182, 162.

W.

Waddell, J. A. L., 132.
Wainwright, Mr., 140.

Walker, R. J., on J., 40.
Wasson, Mr., 124, 139.
Watanabe, 163.
Webster, Daniel, service in J. Expedition, 40, 112.
Weddel, Lord, in J., 19.
Wertheimber on J., 148.
Whalers, wrecks of, 35, 37.
Wheeler, Wm., 136, 137.
Whitman, C. O., 125.
Whitney, Dr., N. W., 126; Prof. W. D., 141.
William II. of Holland, letter of, to J., 22, 82.
Williams, Geo. B., 139.
Williams, Dr. W. S., visits J., 32, 47; on Perry Expedition, 113, 115; on Harris, 115; on Western influence in J., 151.
Woman, education of J., 154, 179-183.
Woolsey, T. D., 118.

X.

Xavier, Fancis, mission in J., 10.

Y.

Yale University, 167.
Yamakawa, 171.
Yatabe, 172.
Yedo, see Tokyo.
Yesso, see Hokkaido.
Yokohama, foreign trade in, 69.
Yoshida, Torajiro, 159.
Yoshiwara, 172.
Young, J. R., on American policy in the East, 99; travels with Grant, 146; on House, 147.

Z.

Zadkiel, Prophet, on J., 44.

JOHNS HOPKINS UNIVERSITY STUDIES
IN
Historical and Political Science.
HERBERT B. ADAMS, Editor.

FIRST SERIES.—Local Institutions.—1883.

I. An Introduction to American Institutional History. By EDWARD A. FREEMAN. 25 cents.
II. The Germanic Origin of New England Towns. By H. B. ADAMS. 50 cents.
III. Local Government in Illinois. By ALBERT SHAW.—Local Government in Pennsylvania. By E. R. L. GOULD. 30 cents.
IV. Saxon Tithingmen in America. By H. B. ADAMS. 50 cents.
V. Local Government in Michigan, and the Northwest. By E. W. BEMIS. 25 cents.
VI. Parish Institutions of Maryland. By EDWARD INGLE. 40 cents.
VII. Old Maryland Manors. By JOHN HEMSLEY JOHNSON. 30 cents.
VIII. Norman Constables in America. By H. B. ADAMS. 50 cents.
IX-X. Village Communities of Cape Ann and Salem. By H. B. ADAMS. 50 cents.
XI. The Genesis of a New England State (Connecticut). By ALEXANDER JOHNSTON. 30 cents.
XII. Local Government and Free Schools in South Carolina. By B. J. RAMAGE. 40 cents.

SECOND SERIES.—Institutions and Economics.—1884.

I-II. Methods of Historical Study. By H. B. ADAMS. 50 cents.
III. The Past and the Present of Political Economy. By R. T. ELY. 35 cents.
IV. Samuel Adams, The Man of the Town Meeting. By JAMES K. HOSMER. 35 cents.
V-VI. Taxation in the United States. By HENRY CARTER ADAMS. 50 cents.
VII. Institutional Beginnings in a Western State. By JESSE MACY. 25 cents.
VIII-IX. Indian Money as a Factor in New England Civilization. By WILLIAM B. WEEDEN. 50 cents.
X. Town and County Government in the English Colonies of North America. By EDWARD CHANNING. 50 cents.
XI. Rudimentary Society among Boys. By J. HEMSLEY JOHNSON. 50 cents.
XII. Land Laws of Mining Districts. By C. H. SHINN. 50 cents.

THIRD SERIES.—Maryland, Virginia and Washington.—1885.

I. Maryland's Influence upon Land Cessions to the United States. George Washington's Interest in Western Lands, the Potomac Company, and a National University. By H. B. ADAMS. 75 cents.
II-III. Virginia Local Institutions:—The Land System; Hundred; Parish; County; Town. By E. INGLE. 75 cents.
IV. Recent American Socialism. By RICHARD T. ELY. 50 cents.
V-VI-VII. Maryland Local Institutions:—The Land System; Hundred; County; Town. By LEWIS W. WILHELM. $1.00.

VIII. The Influence of the Proprietors in Founding the State of New Jersey. By AUSTIN SCOTT. 25 cents.
IX-X. American Constitutions; The Relations of the Three Departments as Adjusted by a Century. By HORACE DAVIS. 50 cents.
XI-XII. The City of Washington. By J. A. PORTER. 50 cents.

FOURTH SERIES.—Municipal Government and Land Tenure.—1886.

I. Dutch Village Communities on the Hudson River. By IRVING ELTING. 50 cents.
II-III. Town Government in Rhode Island. By W. E. FOSTER.—The Narragansett Planters. By EDWARD CHANNING. 50 cents.
IV. Pennsylvania Boroughs. By WILLIAM P. HOLCOMB. 50 cents.
V. Introduction to the Constitutional and Political History of the individual States. By J. F. JAMESON. 50 cents.
VI. The Puritan Colony at Annapolis, Maryland. By DANIEL R. RANDALL. 50 cents.
VII-VIII-IX. History of the Land Question in the United States. By SHOSUKE SATO. $1.00.
X. The Town and City Government of New Haven. By CHARLES H. LEVERMORE. 50 cents.
XI-XII. The Land System of the New England Colonies. By MELVILLE EGLESTON. 50 cents.

FIFTH SERIES.—Municipal Government, History and Politics.—1887.

I-II. City Government of Philadelphia. By EDWARD P. ALLINSON and BOIES PENROSE. 50 cents.
III. City Government of Boston. By JAMES M. BUGBEE. 25 cents.
IV. City Government of St. Louis. By MARSHALL S. SNOW. 25 cents.
V-VI. Local Government in Canada. By JOHN GEORGE BOURINOT. 50 cents.
VII. The Influence of the War of 1812 upon the Consolidation of the American Union. By NICHOLAS MURRAY BUTLER. 25 cents.
VIII. Notes on the Literature of Charities. By HERBERT B. ADAMS. 25 cents.
IX. The Predictions of Hamilton and De Tocqueville. By JAMES BRYCE. 25 cents.
X. The Study of History in England and Scotland. By PAUL FREDERICQ. 25 cents.
XI. Seminary Libraries and University Extension. By H. B. ADAMS. 25 cents.
XII. European Schools of History and Politics. By ANDREW D. WHITE. 25 cents.

SIXTH SERIES.—The History of Co-operation in the United States.—1888.

SEVENTH SERIES.—Social Science, Education, and Government.—1889.

I. Arnold Toynbee. By F. C. MONTAGUE. With an Account of the Work of Toynbee Hall in East London, by PHILIP LYTTELTON GELL. 50 cents.
II-III. The Establishment of Municipal Government in San Francisco. By BERNARD MOSES. 50 cents.
IV. The City Government of New Orleans. By WILLIAM W. HOWE. 25 cents.
V-VI. English Culture in Virginia: A Study of the Gilmer Letters, etc. By WILLIAM P. TRENT. $1.00.

VII-VIII-IX. The River Towns of Connecticut. Wethersfield, Hartford and Windsor. By CHARLES M. ANDREWS. $1.50.

X-XI-XII. Federal Government in Canada. By JOHN G. BOURINOT. $1.00.

EIGHTH SERIES.—History, Politics, and Education.—
1890.—Subscription, $3.00.

I-II. The Beginnings of American Nationality. The Constitutional Relations between the Continental Congress and the Colonies and States. By ALBION W. SMALL, Ph. D. (J. H. U.), President of Colby University. $1.00.

III. Local Government in Wisconsin. By DAVID E. SPENCER, A. B., Instructor in History, University of Wisconsin. 25 cents.

IV. Spanish Colonization in the Southwest. By FRANK W. BLACKMAR, Ph. D., Professor of History and Sociology in the University of Kansas. 50 cents.

V-VI. The Study of History in Germany and France. By Professor PAUL FREDERICQ, of the University of Ghent. Translated by Henrietta Leonard, A. B. (Smith College). $1.00.

VII-VIII-IX. Progress of the Colored People of Maryland since the War. By JEFFREY R. BRACKETT, Ph. D. $1.00.

X. The Study of History in Belgium and Holland. By Professor PAUL FREDERICQ. 50 cents.

XI-XII. Seminary Notes on Recent Historical Literature. By H. B. ADAMS, J. M. VINCENT, W. B. SCAIFE, Ph. D. (Vienna) and others.

EXTRA VOLUMES.

I. THE REPUBLIC OF NEW HAVEN. A History of Municipal Evolution. By Professor CHARLES H. LEVERMORE, Ph. D. 342 pages, 8o. Cloth, $2.00.

II. PHILADELPHIA, 1681-1887. A History of Municipal Development. By EDWARD P. ALLINSON, A. M., and BOIES PENROSE, A. B. 444 pages, 8o. Cloth, $3.00.

III. BALTIMORE AND THE NINETEENTH OF APRIL, 1861. A Study of the War. By GEORGE WILLIAM BROWN, Chief Judge of the Supreme Bench of Baltimore and Mayor of the City in 1861. 176 pages, 8o. Cloth, $1.00.

IV-V. LOCAL CONSTITUTIONAL HISTORY OF THE UNITED STATES. By Professor GEORGE E. HOWARD.
Vol. I.—Development of the Township, Hundred, and Shire. 498 pages, 8o. Cloth, $3.00.
Vol. II.—Development of the City and the Local Magistracies (in press).

VI. THE NEGRO IN MARYLAND. A Study of the Institution of Slavery. By JEFFREY R. BRACKETT, Ph. D. 270 pages, 8o. Cloth, $2.00.

VII. THE SUPREME COURT OF THE UNITED STATES. Its History and Influence in our Constitutional History. By W. W. WILLOUGHBY, A. B. 124 pages, 8o. Cloth, $1.25.

VIII. THE INTERCOURSE BETWEEN THE UNITED STATES AND JAPAN. By INAZO NITOBE.

NOTES SUPPLEMENTARY TO THE STUDIES.

The publication of this series of *Notes* was begun in January, 1889. The following have thus far been issued:

MUNICIPAL GOVERNMENT IN ENGLAND. By Dr. ALBERT SHAW of Minneapolis.

SOCIAL WORK IN AUSTRALIA AND LONDON. By Mr. WILLIAM GREY, of the Denison Club, London.

ENCOURAGEMENT OF HIGHER EDUCATION. By Professor HERBERT B. ADAMS.

THE PROBLEM OF CITY GOVERNMENT. By Hon. SETH LOW, President of Columbia College.

THE LIBRARIES OF BALTIMORE. By Mr. P. R. UHLER, of the Peabody Institute.

WORK AMONG THE WORKINGWOMEN IN BALTIMORE. By Professor HERBERT B. ADAMS.

CHARITIES: THE RELATION OF THE STATE, THE CITY, AND THE INDIVIDUAL TO MODERN PHILANTHROPIC WORK. By A. G. WARNER, Ph. D., Associate Professor in the University of Nebraska.

LAW AND HISTORY. By Dr. WALTER B. SCAIFE, Reader on Historical Geography in the Johns Hopkins University.

THE NEEDS OF SELF-SUPPORTING WOMEN. By Miss CLARE DE GRAFFENRIED, of the Department of Labor, Washington, D. C.

THE ENOCH PRATT FREE LIBRARY OF BALTIMORE. By Dr. L. H. STEINER, Librarian of the Pratt Library.

EARLY PRESBYTERIANISM IN MARYLAND. By Rev. J. W. MCILVAIN, of Baltimore.

EDUCATIONAL ASPECT OF THE U. S. NATIONAL MUSEUM. By Prof. OTIS T. MASON.

These Notes are sent without charge to regular subscribers to the Studies. They are sold at five cents each; twenty-five copies will be furnished for $1.00.

The set of eight volumes is now offered in a handsome library edition for $24.00.

The eight volumes, with seven extra volumes, "New Haven," "Baltimore," "Philadelphia," "Local Constitutional History," Vol. I, "Negro in Maryland," "U. S. Supreme Court," and "U. S. and Japan," altogether twelve volumes, for $33.00.

The seven extra volumes (now ready) will be furnished together for $10.50.

All business communications should be addressed to THE JOHNS HOPKINS PRESS, BALTIMORE, MARYLAND. Subscriptions will also be received, or single copies furnished by any of the following

AMERICAN AGENTS:

New York.—G. P. Putnam's Sons, 27 W. 23d St.
New Haven.—E. P. Judd.
Boston.—Damrell & Upham; W. B. Clarke & Co.
Providence.—Tibbitts & Preston.
Philadelphia.—Porter & Coates; J. B. Lippincott Co.
Washington.—W. H. Lowdermilk & Co.; Brentano's.
Baltimore.—John Murphy & Co.; Cushing & Co.
Cincinnati.—Robert Clarke & Co.
Indianapolis.—Bowen-Merrill Co.
Chicago.—A. C. McClurg & Co.
Louisville.—Flexner & Staadeker.
San Francisco.—Bancroft Company.
New Orleans.—George F. Wharton.
Richmond.—Randolph & English.
Toronto.—Carswell & Co.
Montreal.—William Foster Brown & Co.

EUROPEAN AGENTS:

London.—Kegan Paul, Trench, Trübner & Co.; G. P. Putnam's Sons.
Paris.—A. Hermann, 8 rue de la Sorbonne; Em. Terquem, 31bis Boulevard Haussmann.
Strassburg.—Karl J. Trübner.
Berlin.—Puttkammer & Mühlbrecht; Mayer & Müller.
Leipzig.—F. A. Brockhaus.
Frankfort.—Joseph Baer & Co.
Turin, Florence, and Rome.—E. Loescher.

www.ingramcontent.com/pod-product-compliance
Lightning Source LLC
Chambersburg PA
CBHW020859230426
43666CB00008B/1237